"Hurley and Dobson's newest book offers many subtle insights into the personality types, and their theories point to new directions well worth investigating. They are doing fine, original work in this field."

DON RICHARD RISO
author of *Personality Types*

"My Best Self will propel you to the very center of your soul. Light years beyond mere personality typing, Hurley and Dobson illuminate the psychospiritual journey with profound insights from the Enneagram, Christian spirituality, and neuroscience research. Absolutely required reading for those committed to healing the self and the world."

LEN SPERRY, M.D., PH.D.
professor of psychiatry
Medical College of Wisconsin

"Seldom do authors combine clear thinking with soul work and Spirit all at the same time. Hurley and Dobson have moved Enneagram studies to a new level of creativity and practicality at the same time. If the Enneagram has already changed your life, these insights will add feeling, freedom, and flight."

RICHARD ROHR, O.F.M
author of *Discovering the Enneagram*

"Kathy Hurley and Ted Dobson now reveal a vastly new understanding of the Enneagram's power. It is more than a personality typing system, it is about *reclaiming the human soul.* This book is a must for those who seek to broaden and cultivate their relationship with God, with themselves, and with the universe."

BARBARA SHLEMON RYAN
former chairwoman of the Association of Christian Therapists, and author of *Healing the Hidden Self*

My Best Self

Using the Enneagram
to Free the Soul

Kathleen V. Hurley
Theodore E. Dobson

HarperSanFrancisco
A Division of HarperCollinsPublishers

From Kathy:

In grateful memory of Mildred Walker,
my mom,
my heroine, my adversary,
and unquestionably a woman of the earth
and a woman of faith

From Ted:

To my dad, Ted,
whose feeling for his wife and his children,
curiosity about life and dedication to his art,
and love of his family and friends
continue to inspire me and make me grateful

FIRST EDITION

Library of Congress Cataloging-in-Publication Data

Hurley, Kathleen V.
My best self : using the enneagram to free the soul /
Kathleen V. Hurley, Theodore E. Dobson. – 1st ed.
p. cm.
Includes bibliographical references.

ISBN 0–06–250332–4 (alk. paper)

1. Enneagram. I. Dobson, Theodore E. II. Title.
BF698.35.E54H87 1993
155.2′6—dc20   92–53922

99 00 01 02 RRD-H 10 9 8

Contents

Introduction

Enneagram Riddles

---

*God sets nothing but riddles. Here
the boundaries meet and all
contradictions exist side by side.*
—FYODOR DOSTOYEVSKI
Brothers Karamazov

This book on the Enneagram is unlike anything we could have imagined writing even two years ago. It's not another presentation of the nine personality types that the Enneagram describes, although we do briefly explain the nine types (in chapter 1), both to introduce them for people new to the system and also to probe more insightfully into the unconscious motivation of each type for those already familiar with its extraordinary power to explain human personality. Neither is this a book that will simply add details to the system, applying its wisdom to this kind of situation or that type of activity.

This is a book with an entirely new perspective on the Enneagram, a perspective that originates in probing questions and puzzling riddles.

Among the questions to be probed is one that we have been asked in every seminar we have presented on the

Enneagram: How did the patterned behaviors of each of the nine personality types originate? The accuracy of the Enneagram in describing the unconscious, or mechanical, quality to many of our responses in life is obvious to even the newest student of this wisdom. Thus, the next obvious question is, If this is the way I am, how did I get to be this way?

These aren't idle questions, either; as we delve into them in this book, we'll see these questions contain wisdom for neutralizing our compulsions and pointing us toward freedom. Another question often asked in Enneagram seminars is, Once I become consciously aware of both my weaknesses and my strengths, what are the positive choices I can make to maximize the gifts and talents inherent in my personality?

The Enneagram does more than draw out questions like these, however. It also poses riddles about human nature that press the inquisitive mind for a response. The challenge of these questions and many others gives rise to exciting new insights that continue to yield a profound wisdom for living a healthy life.

A riddle, according to the dictionary, is "a mystifying, misleading, or puzzling question posed as a problem to be solved or guessed: something difficult to understand." Life itself, then, could be seen as the greatest riddle of all, created by a Master Riddle Maker. And what a wonderful riddle—difficult, but not impossible, to understand!

Have we mistakenly been misled by a false notion that life is a problem to be solved rather than a question to be lived, a mystery inviting lifelong exploration? Many personal situations, as well as global conditions, do indeed appear to be problems, problems impossible to solve. If, however, they were looked upon as riddles (questions posed as problems), could the same conditions be turned into important opportunities—life lessons that, if experienced and understood, might move us closer to resolving the great riddle? In this book we'll approach some of these broader issues of life, culture, transformation, and change, and we'll discover that the Enneagram and the psycho-spirituality that undergirds it has much to say to us today.

What Is the Enneagram?

Everyone who begins to explore human behavior becomes aware of the beauty and the mystery that permeates the personality of every person. The teaching of the Enneagram, long a secret wisdom (and only in this century made available to a public whose quest for human values grows in urgency with every passing year), gives order and coherence to what at first appears to be a marvelous but disorganized mosaic of human potential.

From the Greek *enneas,* meaning "nine," and *grammos,* meaning "points," the Enneagram presents nine personality patterns arranged in a diagram as points around a circle. The Enneagram tells us that people with each of these nine personality types live with an unconscious motivation that causes them to respond to life in a way so consistent as to become the driving force shaping their lives. This unconscious motivation gives each type a unique understanding of life, people, and the world.

Further, the Enneagram says that each person has three different kinds, or centers, of intelligence. The three centers are often overlooked by students of the Enneagram, who quickly become intrigued by the insightful descriptions of the nine personality types. However, we have come to realize that hidden in the description of the Enneagram's three centers of intelligence lies the essence of an invaluable wisdom for life; therefore, the three centers will develop as the central theme of this book.[1]

Substantiated in the brain research of the last half of this century, these centers of intelligence correspond to those of the three-brain theory commonly accepted in scientific circles. The Intellectual Center (the neocortex) has the role of thinking, abstracting, and objectifying. The Relational Center (the emotional or mammalian brain) processes our emotions and understands the human-relational dimension of life; it is also the seat of the ego. The Creative Center (the physical or reptilian brain) understands the physical world; from it we get our sense of how to deal with that world.

The three centers of intelligence are more fully explained in chapter 2, but we can say here that the Enneagram teaches that each personality type learns to prefer or overuse one center of intelligence. This dimension of intelligence becomes the predominant source for understanding life and interacting with others and the world. A second center becomes a supporting intelligence

---

[1]Throughout this book, we use the phrases "three centers of intelligence" and "three centers" interchangeably.

that the person uses freely, while the third center of intelligence remains underused, dormant, repressed.

The interconnecting relationship intended for the three centers can be pictured as a small musical ensemble of three players and instruments. In a good ensemble, the musicians modulate their tone so as to keep the music balanced and harmonized, with no instrument overpowering the others. Though each musician is often featured in a solo performance, no one instrument continually occupies center stage.

In a disunified group whose members are competitive with each other, however, one musician often plays too loud and takes all solo performances, whether or not that person's instrument is suited to the music. As often happens in any group of three, when one dominates, another follows, and the third party is ignored and so becomes disgruntled and eventually leaves. Following our analogy of a musical trio, while the second player allows the first to take over, the third may become bored and play halfheartedly or simply depart. It's not as if the group doesn't make music—of course it does—but the music isn't harmonious, and the discord among the musicians becomes more obvious as time goes on.

A similar kind of imbalance and discord happens in our inner ensemble of three centers of intelligence. One center plays too loud and too long, disrupting the harmony of our lives. Like the overbearing musician, this center becomes preferred and overworked and claims center stage in our lives. This overused intelligence, then, has too much influence in shaping our personality and in determining the way we respond to life and to people.

One of the other two centers takes its cue from the lead player and learns to follow even the most subtle variation on the theme of our life. In so doing, this center develops an unusually high quality of versatility and expertise. Our final player, however, the third center of intelligence, is ignored. It becomes disgruntled and abandons us. Because its purpose is unfamiliar to us, it appears both useless and unimportant.

New Riddles for the Enneagram

One of the most captivating aspects of Enneagram wisdom is its paradoxes: certain seeming contradictions that invite curious and imaginative seekers on a spiraling path toward understanding. We have come to love these contradictions, for they have challenged us to think, to ponder, and to explore. In a world in which almost everything is prepared or premixed and prepackaged for our convenience—a world, for example, in which the technology of television lulls our creative imagination to sleep by presenting us with stories and pictures simultaneously—the riddles of life are experiences to be cherished, for they awaken our slumbering potential to form, impregnate, and guide our own destiny.

For centuries, the Enneagram was an oral teaching. As this tradition was handed down to us, one of the paradoxes of the system involved three (of the nine) Enneagram types that are called the Balance Point Numbers: the Three, the Six, and the Nine.

It is commonly taught that the personality of each type is primarily shaped by overusing one center of intelligence, which is then preferred over the other two. The oral tradition then states that the Balance Point Numbers *repressed* the very intelligence they also *preferred*—indeed a puzzling notion when you think about what it means. How can you overuse and underuse the same intelligence simultaneously?

The oral tradition used this seeming contradiction to explain how these three types maintained their unique approach to living. For they are said to try to keep their responses to life in balance with other people's responses and with the world. But the question remains: If personality is formed by one intelligence taking center stage, which intelligence forms the personalities of the Balance Point Numbers? This question has created the riddle that has pursued and challenged us throughout the years.

Our desire to understand what made these numbers tick was possibly amplified because one of us (Kathy) is one of the Balance Point Numbers, a Three. How can these patterns overuse and underuse one center of intelligence at the same time? became an irresistible question that we pursued as intently as it pursued us.

The riddle of the Balance Points. As you look at the Enneagram, these Balance Point Numbers are obviously connected by a self-contained equilateral triangle; the lines in the Enneagram that connect them are cut off from the other six numbers. (See the diagram titled "The Enneagram.") In the literature explaining the Enneagram by its first teachers in the West, this aspect of it is known as the Law of Three: the recurring decimals created by dividing three by one, two, and three.[2]

These numbers are each in the middle of a center (Relational, Intellectual, and Creative) and prefer and repress the same center. (See the diagram titled "The Centers.") Because centers are types of intelligence or ways of perceiving and dealing with the world, this notion that a person could prefer and repress the same one confused us. Although this idea was commonly taught and accepted, we never found it interpreted clearly. In a vague way we attempted to decipher what it meant in our seminars, but neither logic nor intuition could yield a clear understanding of what this teaching is intended to convey.

The other six types preferred one center and repressed another. The logic of this concept was perfectly clear to us; with careful study we began to see how many aspects of the descriptions of these numbers could be easily explained and understood because they prefer one center of intelligence and repress a different center of intelligence.

The confusion that surrounded the Balance Point Numbers and prevented a clear understanding of these types became the riddle that enticed us to travel the strange and wonderful path that was to become this book.

Since the first time we were exposed to the Enneagram

---

[2]For example, see John G. Bennett, *Enneagram Studies* (York Beach, ME: Samuel Weiser, 1983), pp. 2–3. The Law of Three is complemented by the Law of Seven, which is created by dividing seven by all the numerals below it. Each of these calculations also creates a recurring decimal that explains the broken line that connects the other six types of the Enneagram.

we intuitively recognized that we had come in contact with a powerful form of truth. The excitement that was ignited in that initial experience has matured over the ensuing decade into a passionate confidence that because the Enneagram is a wisdom that we in the West had just begun to explore, it must continue to grow, unfold, and change. As we began to examine it more closely, we found that it presented other riddles as well. The next riddle surfaced in the three centers of intelligence.

The riddle of the centers.   The Enneagram claims that every person has three equally important intelligences: thinking, feeling, and doing. This is an understanding of human nature that flies in the face of commonly accepted assumptions, for in Western civilization intelligence is generally identified with thinking alone. Yet, in examining the scientific understanding of the human brain gleaned during this century, we found astounding corroboration for this ancient philosophy describing the three centers of intelligence. Results from modern scientific studies, which we briefly summarize in chapter 2, undergird the Enneagram on every major point.

What the Enneagram describes, however, is nine *compulsive* personality patterns that are based in an *overuse* of one of the three kinds of intelligence. If bringing the personality to maturity is based not in overuse but proper use, what would these three centers of intelligence look like if they were expressed purely? Clues to resolving this Enneagram riddle first came to us from a mysterious and amazing source.

The Enneagram

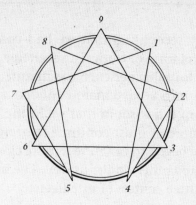

The Centers

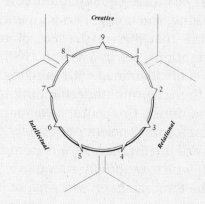

Intuitive Knowledge from a Dream

Throughout history, certain individuals have experienced unexplainable flashes of knowledge. Whether through dreams, intuition, inner vision, or a flash of insight, these people suddenly found themselves in possession of complex concepts. Because the ideas are new—not simply a product of the process of rational deduction—this unexpected "knowing" cannot be explained logically.

Probably the most celebrated example of this kind of knowledge is Einstein's theory of relativity. Einstein reported that the equation $E = mc^2$ came to him in a dream he had in his twenties, and he spent the next two decades figuring out the logical and mathematical reasoning behind it.

What is the source of information like this? According to one psychological theory, that of the Swiss psychologist C. G. Jung, it rises from a collective level of the unconscious mind—a level of awareness that is common to all human beings, that contains deep wisdom, and that is open to Spirit. Religions call the same experience divine revelation or inspiration.

In the wisdom surrounding and undergirding the Enneagram, knowledge that comes this way is understood as coming from higher worlds. A crack or fissure opens up through all levels of matter, and through this crack ordinary people may, for a short time, perceive or receive new perceptions from the higher worlds. The information is received as a nonrational perception of preexisting knowledge.[3]

---

[3]Philosophical systems endeavor to explain all of reality, and this experience, though relatively uncommon in Western culture (but much more common in civilizations that do not overvalue the rational mind), is a part of recorded human experience. Most philosophies, therefore, have theories on the origins of this kind of knowledge. Plato, for example, taught about Divine Ideas that were the source of all material reality and could be contacted by certain individuals. Even philosophers as dedicated to rational thought as Thomas Aquinas made room in their thinking for "nonconceptual knowledge."

The night of February 4, 1989, I (Kathy) experienced my own version of this sort of revelation through a dream. Even as I slept, I knew I was broadening and deepening my current understanding of the Enneagram.

The dream began with a recounting of my life from a spiritual perspective, using the image of crossing a river to portray the first half of my life. After that part was finished, I awoke and saw that it was 4:13 A.M. The rest of the experience as I recorded it the following morning was as follows:

For no logical reason I remember thinking that three plus one equals four, but that only gave me two fours, and there needed to be one more before it was complete. I lay there for a while thinking about the dream before finally drifting back into sleep.

Then I heard a man say, "Now I will interpret your dream for you." I thought that would be great, so I waited for him to continue. There was a long pause before he started to speak again. This time he said, "Now I will interpret the Creed for you." I thought that was strange because it wasn't what he said the first time, but I didn't say anything, and he continued:

"All people on earth are children of the Father/Mother, the Healer, or the Spirit. By one of these they have been created, protected, and nurtured.

"You are a child of the Spirit. The Spirit's children are given the gifts of new ideas, possibilities, and unrealized concepts. Water is their symbol. *Water flows through them, not to them.* They live in the mind first, the physical realm second, and the heart third. Dining on crystal dishes, they are sustained by the intangible. Sojourns in the spiritual dimension, intuition or mental meandering, and pondering are their natural resources.

"The Healer's children are given the gifts of incarnation, synthesizing, and integrating. Fire is their symbol. *They carry the flame but cannot contain the flame.* They live in the heart first, the mind second, and the physical realm third. Dining on fine china, they are sustained by the intangible becoming tangible. Making the invisible visible through words, feeling and integration are their natural resources.

"The children of the Father/Mother are given the gifts of guidance, development, and completion. The earth is their symbol. *They belong to the earth, but the earth does not belong to them.* They live in the physical realm first, the heart second, and the mind third. Dining on pottery, they are sustained by the abundance of the earth. Abilities to access the material, an innate sense of timing, and innovation are their natural resources.

"Children of the Spirit initiate, children of the Healer incarnate, and children of the Father/Mother complete—initiation (Spring), incarnation (Summer), completion (Fall).

"Although all people are given the ability to survive in this world, unless they unite with and companion the other two, their life journey will be a tormented survival. A tortured body and heart will plague the child of the Spirit. A tortured mind and body will plague the child of the Healer. A tortured heart and mind will plague the child of the Father/Mother. Through selfless surrender to others, the happiness of heaven is available to all."

At this point I asked a question. "How do we know whose child we are?"

The answer: "All people carry the image of their parent within. If they search, they will—without doubt, without question—know. The child of the Spirit and the child of the Healer must bond with each other. Then together they must bond with the child of the Father/Mother. It is this triune bonding that will yield the fourth and final companion needed to release the human spirit to transcend the limitations of the human. *That* is the Creed.

"Before any of this is possible, however, each person is required to learn the lessons of the other two realms. Through that process, one comes to respect and value the life cycles of the other two."

After this explanation, the voice interpreted the personal part of the dream for me. Then he said, "You've reached the other side of the river. Now the journey must begin."

I awakened alert and knowing I must immediately record the dream or I would lose all recollection of it. I sat up looking at the clock. It was 4:44 A.M. and I said aloud, "And now there are twelve."

The riddles of the dream. For the next two years we struggled to understand just how the dream applied to the Enneagram. Interpreting symbols sometimes takes much thought, reflection, and questioning, especially when—as these did—they arise from the collective unconscious. Further, it has been our experience that symbols take on added meaning with time as new events, study, and dialogue expand one's awareness of their underlying meaning.

The interpretation of the first part of the dream, though at first it appeared complete in itself, concluded with the enigmatic statement "Now the journey must begin." Even though in the first part of the dream I (Kathy) had just been through a long and perilous journey crossing the river, the interpreter says, "Now the journey must begin." What could that mean? It was in attempting to answer this new riddle that our awareness of the deeper meaning of the Enneagram began to emerge.

Regarding the Enneagram, we understood that "Children of the Spirit" would apply to those people who preferred the Intellectual (thinking) Center; "Children of the Healer" to those people who preferred the Relational (feeling) Center; and "Children of the Father/Mother" to those people who preferred the Creative (doing) Center.

The description of the gifts and natural resources of each "child" broadened and deepened our understanding of the importance of each center of intelligence. With reflection and study we could clearly see why it is so important to develop each center—not only for the healthy maturing of the person, but also for the well-being and healthy development of society as a whole.

The implications of this understanding, though potentially quite powerful, seemed questionable, however, because for a Three—a Succeeder—the Preferred Center is the Relational Center, not the Intellectual Center. Yet, the interpreter had clearly stated to Kathy, who is a Three, "You are a child of the Spirit," which would indicate that the Intellectual Center predominates in her life.

It was a riddle that appeared to have no solution until early in 1991. We had been working on developing a new, advanced seminar on the Enneagram. For months we had talked, read, and filled notebooks with ideas and possibilities that had been flooding our minds. We were under pressure because we had committed ourselves to present a *new* Enneagram seminar. Although the date was rapidly approaching, we had no idea of what we might do or what direction we might take.

In desperation, we decided to spend an entire day silently reading through the piles of notes taken during the previous months as we explored various possible approaches. Our intention was to allow the material of our prior research to seep beneath the level of logic. Perhaps by not trying to talk it through or figure it out, we would encourage a new and fresh insight to break through to our conscious minds.

Seven silent hours had passed when suddenly everything fell into place. We felt as if we were understanding the wisdom of the Enneagram for the first time! After the initial moment of "Aha!" we realized that the riddle contained in the Enneagram dream was now at least beginning to be solved. It may take a lifetime, however, to understand its meaning fully—and even a lifetime may not be long enough.

What we came to realize in that moment and have begun to explore in this book is that *the Enneagram is much more than a personality typing system!* If you choose to limit it to personality, you can gain important and helpful perspectives on yourself and others, but you will miss the real point, power, and purpose of this wisdom.

What is that purpose? The Enneagram is about unity within oneself and among human beings. It's about healing the hidden pain of life. It teaches us how to release the power and creative energy to follow our destiny, and through it we discover what gives us life. *The Enneagram is about soul making.*

Condensing this deeper and wider understanding of the power of the Enneagram for human happiness and wholeness, we drew out some of the essential elements of the dream and reformulated them into the following riddle:

An Enneagram Riddle of Restoration

*When One becomes nine
Then nine become twelve,
When two become three
Then three become four,
When four become one
Then one becomes all,
When all become One
The riddle is solved.*

This Enneagram Riddle contains the flickering lights of sacred questions that hold the possibility of guiding us into the land of light and shadow that is soul making. Soul making is a process of reflection and action, of thinking, feeling, and doing in freedom and creativity. It is our hope that this book will be a guide in understanding a little more clearly the process of soul making. We will attempt to resolve some of the mysterious questions hidden beneath and beyond the surface of the riddle and of the Enneagram.

Now that the book is complete, we can say that the process of writing it was wonderfully exciting and stimulating. Though that is true, it's also true that we were often struggling through frustration, irritation, and insecurity. Our quest for understanding has led us to turn many commonly accepted views of life and of the Enneagram—our own and others'—inside out and upside down. On each step of the way it seemed a new question would rise up to challenge some long-held belief or idea, or we would be led into an area of life we never wanted to explore. Thus, like life, this process has been a winding path through hills and vales that, in retrospect, we would happily travel again, for it has led us through the mysterious and ever-changing sacred land of soul.

All who have ever questioned the meaning of their own life are invited to walk with us on the wildly passionate and beautiful journey of soul making through the Enneagram.

1

Soul Making
and the Enneagram

—————

*There are no ordinary people. You have
never talked to a mere mortal. Nations,
cultures, arts, civilizations—these are
mortal, and their life is to ours as the
life of a gnat. But it is immortals whom
we joke with, work with, marry, snub,
and exploit—immortal horrors or
everlasting splendors.*

—C. S. LEWIS
"The Weight of Glory"

We are living in exciting and perilous times. In the
world today there is a rapidly awakening desire for spiritual understanding. The longing for honesty, sincerity,
and truth has been quietly growing in the generative
depths of individuals and nations. Now, this previously
hidden desire to understand what is valuable and meaningful in life is emerging from the silent womb of society.

Why is this interest growing at such an amazing rate
at this point in history? Both religious and secular

prophets have put forth a variety of explanations ranging from fear of impending doom and destruction to hope for the birth of a utopian paradise.

All you have to do, however, is look beneath the surface of Western society over the last half century to see that dramatic shifts in attitudes, values, and ideals have been taking place. Commentators in fields as diverse as science and theology, philosophy and pop culture, sociology and ecology, art and psychology have been observing these trends—at an ever-accelerating rate.[1] Now, in this last decade of the century and the millennium, a heightening awareness of our values as a society has exploded in modern consciousness. In a fast-changing sociopolitical and economic structure, we are reexamining our values and finding them wanting.

Strangely enough, it is the very lack of values sometimes celebrated by our culture that has regenerated this reassessment. We live in an age of information in which everyone can have, as Andy Warhol phrased it, fifteen minutes of fame; consequently, we have seen hollow he-

------

[1]By the middle decades of the twentieth century paleontologist and theologian Pierre Teilhard de Chardin, psychologist and philosopher C. G. Jung, and philosopher and theologian Rodney Collin were observing this movement in the deep undercurrents of Western civilization, each from his own scientific and epistemological perspectives. Since then, the list has grown to encompass individuals from a wide range of fields, including (and this list is meant to be illustrative, not comprehensive) sociological observer John Naisbitt, theologian Matthew Fox, English poet Kathleen Raine, pop culture commentator Marilyn Ferguson, psychologist Robert Johnson, mystic Thomas Merton, and mythologist Joseph Campbell.

The Enneagram

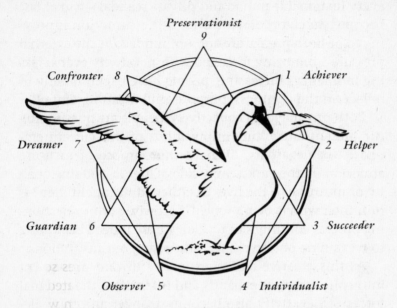

Preservationist
9

Confronter 8   1 *Achiever*

Dreamer 7   2 *Helper*

Guardian 6   3 *Succeeder*

Observer 5   4 *Individualist*

This diagram is based upon one in *Enneagram Studies* by John G. Bennett (York Beach, Maine: Samuel Weiser, Inc., 1974), p. 3. The design and the names that are assigned to each number are original to Dobson and Hurley.

roes, who melt like chocolate bunnies in the heat of truth, capture the headlines one week and sink into obscurity the next. Daily we are privy to every sordid, intimate detail of degrading behavior that, just a decade ago, would have made us grope for a barf bag. We even learned to eat our family dinners while breathlessly riveted to live scenes from the Gulf War.

It appeared that the general public—bombarded by every imaginable public and private scandal—had at last become shock-proof. However, this assumption is proving to be both premature and unfounded. As the external pressure from being force-fed with negativity every waking moment is increasing, people have begun quietly to reflect on the rightness, purpose, and meaning of it all.

Both privately and collectively, people are questioning the present and future implications of this current emphasis on negativity. "What's the purpose of focusing attention on the dark, seamy side of life? Is it adding quality or meaning to the lives of either adults or children? If not, then who is being served?" Slowly, as this questioning process continues to unfold, we are indeed beginning to reexamine ourselves, our values, and our institutions.

As this creative and questioning inward movement into consciousness expands and intensifies, the external forces of negativity also become stronger and more determined to undermine human dignity. As the tension of these two opposing forces increases, cracks and fissures are opening between the visible and invisible worlds of reality. Through these crevices the winds of change are beginning to blow, and a great giant—the soul of humanity—is stirring.

Thus, although the great giant of soul is stirring, there is also a great giant of hatred waiting to destroy this new consciousness and fight to overpower the soul of humanity. This corrupt giant sucks the lifeblood from society as it feeds on the pain caused by injustice, inequality, greed, fear, insecurity, violence, silence, and repression. Though our focus here will be on the developing of the human soul, we cannot lose touch with reality by forgetting these darker forces. We'll need to become soul makers to deal with the opposing forces of brutality.

The Emerging Wisdom of the Enneagram

In this changing atmosphere it is not surprising that the ancient, long-hidden wisdom of the Enneagram is beginning to rise up and permeate human consciousness. That's because the Enneagram communicates truth in a new way—a way that can be heard in the confusion of the modern world. It's an esoteric wisdom (from the Greek *eso,* "within," and referring to an inner understanding) that doesn't teach new truth but reveals the inner meaning of ageless truth.

The history of this century tells us once again that humanity has become too complacent, too familiar with the common ways of understanding values and morality. These are the foundation upon which cultures can rise above baseness, violence, and self-serving pursuits to become great. Because we have become blind and deaf to the old ways of perceiving truth, the truth of the ages has lost its power to speak to our hearts, to protect new life, or to nurture our souls. Consequently, we are living in exciting and perilous times.

The Enneagram educates us in truth by beginning with our own lives. It pierces illusion and truthfully describes how every person expresses one—and only one—of nine different unconscious motivations that determine what the Enneagram calls the pattern, type, or number of each individual. In this way the Enneagram itself explains the first line of the Enneagram Riddle we referred to in the Introduction, *One becomes nine.* Each personality type is founded on innate strengths, gifts, and talents, but we distort the beauty of our personalities by compulsively overusing our positive attributes.

The reasons we live in this way are presented throughout the pages of this book, but we could summarize them by saying we live much of our lives unconsciously—on automatic pilot, as it were. It's the human condition that, until we become conscious of what's going on in our lives—all our thoughts, feelings, sensations, intuitions, and motivations and the consequences of our actions—we do what we've always done because we've always done it. Truly, this is living in a mechanical way, living like a machine that is programmed to manufacture one and only one product.

We continue to live this way until we wake up to the illusion. Over the years, excessive utilization of our positive attributes creates layers of illusion, enticing us to believe the lie that we've found the road to happiness. Yet how can we be on the road to happiness when depression and stress are so common?

Beyond the descriptions of compulsive personality waits a long-hidden, uncommon wisdom that speaks truth so clearly it unveils the potential for radical goodness in every human being. In doing so it points the way to a path of transformation both for individuals and for society. This wisdom is called The Work. Because the world has reached a point in its evolution when the eyes and ears of its inhabitants need to be reopened, the winds of change, as if preparing us for something new, are leaving traces of this previously secret truth everywhere.

Increasingly—even if not referred to directly as the Enneagram or The Work—this ancient wisdom is appearing in books and magazine articles, being preached from pulpits, being used alongside accepted psychotherapeutic models in counseling offices, and being applied in the business world to improve management and promote team development and for career counseling.[2] Throughout the world, in workshops and seminars, through spiritual direction and in the private lives of spiritual seekers, the collective unconscious appears to be yielding the secret truths of the Enneagram. This heretofore unfamiliar wisdom has the potential to shock us into waking up and recognizing the mechanical, unconscious thinking that prevents us from attaining inner and outer harmony, unity, and freedom.

Because the Enneagram wisdom is a way that is both phenomenological in approach and independent of the traditions of any particular religion, it carries an integrity that makes it compatible with every known system of personal and spiritual understanding. It's this very integrity, however, that causes this wisdom to threaten any person or system that fears individual growth through

---

[2]We first wrote about our ideas on the Enneagram and some principles of The Work in our book *What's My Type?* (San Francisco: Harper San Francisco, 1992). Other books on the Enneagram are also available. Here we are primarily interested in the numbers of books, journals, and articles we have noticed in far-flung and scattered places that rely on the advanced wisdom of The Work.

knowledge, personal responsibility, the freedom to think for oneself, and the development of conscience. Throughout history, limitation of the individual has always been the greatest weapon of repression.

Soul Making

Soul making is central and essential to Enneagram wisdom. Our bodies live in time and space, governed by the material world. By contrast, the human spirit lives in eternal truth. *Only the soul* has the ability to make connection, and therefore establish communication, between spirit and body.

Most people never stop to distinguish between spirit and soul. Among those who have, some may view soul as inferior to spirit. Our need at this crucial time in history is to reexamine these words describing our inner experience to see what they can tell us about ourselves and our resources. Let us, then, explore descriptions and definitions of soul and spirit and take a historical look at these notions.

In the ancient view, spirit refers to the nonmaterial human realm that focuses on eternity, and soul is that nonmaterial human realm that is interested in the things of the earth. Further, although everyone has a soul, soul must be strengthened and stretched to bridge the gap between the spiritual and material worlds. Soul making is the inner journey toward consciousness, wholeness, and healing.

Mechanical, unconscious living rivets the eyes of the soul on the outer world, where it is held hostage by the egocentric demands of the personality. The Enneagram clearly describes the mechanical, compulsive, unconscious behavior that is the expression of the soul in the external world and that finally imprisons it there. The Enneagram also provides the key that can open the prison gates, allowing the eyes of the soul to turn inward, where in searching for honesty, sincerity, and truth the person discovers true freedom.

In a reflective environment soul flourishes, for it is free to search out and discover purpose, personal life meaning, and destiny. The soul, which is grounded in the physical body, can also be set free to soar into the realm of the spirit and return home carrying the golden threads of faith, hope, and love that connect and unite the inner and outer worlds. In this way, the soul can become the Great Bridge between visible and invisible reality. This is the essence of soul making.

As we approach the millennium, the importance of developing one's soul, or soul making, cannot be overemphasized. The Western world—which makes a god out of externalizing everything—has little understanding of the meaning, purpose, or function of the soul. Jung, the eminent Swiss psychologist, recognized this clearly when he said that modern humanity is in search of its soul. Jung can be credited, along with Freud, with bringing this search for soul to the forefront of conscious exploration in modern Western thought.

When did we, as a civilization, lose our awareness of soul, and why is reclaiming an understanding of soul value so critical at this point in our evolution?

For hundreds and hundreds of years, the people of the Western world have been culturally deprived of

understanding how important soul is to attaining wholeness, healing, freedom, and unity. This soul deprivation,
which was taking place in earnest as early as 500 B.C.E.,
became firmly embedded in Western thought in 787 C.E.
at a gathering of the preeminent leaders of the Holy
Catholic Church in Nicaea, in present-day Turkey.[3]

This assembly attempted to resolve the iconoclast (literally, "image breaker") controversy, the often violent
debate that lasted for several centuries about the appro-
priateness of using images in Christian worship of God.
Throughout the ancient world, both in pagan cults and
in Christianity, images of all kinds—paintings, icons,
statues—had been used in worshiping deity. Around the
turning of the eighth century, for many complicated political and religious reasons, the use of images became
suspect, and Emperor Leo III outlawed them.[4]

---

[3]Two councils of the Catholic church were held in the ancient city of
Nicaea. The more famous was the first, held in 325 C.E., which set
down the doctrines that were later to be written in the document
Christians know as the Nicene Creed. This creed summarized the theology that had developed concerning the Persons of the Trinity and
the person and nature of Christ. The council to which we are referring,
Nicea II, was held in the eighth century, and dealt with the use of icons
and other images in Christian worship.

[4]The growing influence of rationalism in the imperial court is cited by
some scholars. Also contributing to the difficulty is the fact that both
Moslems and Jews repudiate the use of images in worship, and in the
Middle East, where Moslems, Jews, and Christians all live alongside
each other, Christians were often called idolatrous image-worshipers.
This issue became political when some emperors and empresses were in
favor of using images, others against, and when the imperial army took
the side of the iconoclasts. Cf. J. D. Conway, *Times of Decision: The Story
of the Councils* (Notre Dame: Fides Publications, 1962), pp. 88–105.

In the resolution of this conflict, the bishops convened at this general council of the Catholic church mediated between those who wanted to sanction the use of images and those who wanted the practice outlawed. They said that images, which are produced by the human imagination and therefore are the most immediate way the soul reveals itself, were appropriate in worship, but *not for their own sake*. Rather, everyone was to understand that the veneration occasioned by images was given to that eternal truth they represented, which lives in the world of spirit.

The relevance of their conclusion on our discussion about the loss of soul is subtle, but important. Soul is not to be appreciated for its own sake, but only for what it reveals about spirit. The long-held understanding of human nature as comprising body, soul, and spirit, with soul and spirit of equal importance, was subtly but lastingly changed. All people in the occidental world, whether or not they are Christian, are affected by the pronouncements of these men over one thousand years ago, for from that day on, soul has slowly been denigrated, put aside, subsumed into spirit, and confused with spirit. Not having its own life, soul has been lost. Finally, in the minds of most people, human nature has been redefined as a material body imbued with a rational, intellectual spirit.

Approximately eighty years later in 869 C.E., a similar gathering of church leaders was convened in Constantinople. The pronouncements of the Second Council of Nicea had not settled the disagreement. All over the Christian world, people repudiated the council's decrees—

from Charlemagne in France and Pope Adrian II in Rome to several of the bishops who were at the council.[5] Again, the controversy was intense and often bloody. By reaffirming the decrees of Nicea II, the participants in the fourth general council of the Catholic church in Constantinople established dualism—the idea that human beings are made up exclusively of spirit (mind) and body (matter)—as the mode of thinking that would control Christianity and the West for centuries to come.[6]

Thus the soul, the anima, which reflects the feminine qualities and virtues of humanity and presents us with images of the feminine Face of God, was banished from the Kingdom, seemingly forever![7] The spirit, which reflects the masculine qualities and virtues of humanity and presents us with masculine images of the Face of God, was given exclusive supremacy in the orthodox

---

[5]Leo Donald Davis, S. J., *The First Seven Ecumenical Councils: Their History and Theology* (Wilmington, Delaware: Michael Glazier, Inc., 1987), pp. 311–12.

[6]Our attention to the importance of these historical facts for psychology, theology, and the future of Western culture was first directed by James Hillman in "Peaks and Vales: The Soul/Spirit Distinction as Basis for the Differences Between Psychotherapy and Spiritual Discipline," in *Puer Papers,* ed. James Hillman (Dallas: Spring Publications, 1979), pp. 54–57. Though we have developed these ideas in our own way, we gratefully acknowledge Hillman's research and contribution to this study.

[7]We use the words *feminine* and *masculine* here in the abstract. We are not referring to male and female human beings but to abstract qualities that can be described as masculine and feminine. From this point of view, every human being is a composite of masculine and feminine qualities—different kinds and of different proportions, to be sure. These qualities can also be seen as values in cultures and civilizations. In this approach we rely on the work of C. G. Jung and his followers.

Christian tradition, the philosophy that has shaped Western thought and society.

Responsibility for the loss of soul understanding cannot be placed exclusively at the feet of the orthodox Christian tradition, however. Society itself, founded as it was on the principles of the Roman Empire, had for centuries elevated the masculine and denigrated the true feminine. The reasons for Western civilization's extroverted approach to life—resulting in contemporary fascination with science, technology, and materialism—cannot be found in any one place. But the Christian church—the keeper of doctrine, the community charged with communicating theological, philosophical, and anthropological truth to Western civilization—became the organ through which this dramatic shift in thinking was most clearly expressed. Thus, it had great influence both on the minds of individuals and on the structures of Western society.

Consequently, it is in the nature of the soul that both our dilemma and our investigation lie. Body and all of matter are the subjects of many sciences. Studied apart from its nonmaterial components, even matter is misunderstood in Western culture.

Spirit, sometimes inappropriately called mind (the dictionary identifies the words *soul, psyche,* and *mind* with one another), is that nonmaterial part of human beings that reaches into the realm of discipline, inspiration, and union with the transcendent Sacred Other. It is tuned into mystery—faith, prayer, visions, revelations, ecstasy, and meditation. It is single-minded in its drive for excellence and is inspired to dedication. Its approach is a movement upward—building and strengthening, searching for the Eternal. It is committed to truth and love, justice and mercy as ways to inspire an experience of the Divine.

Soul is the realm of feeling, emotion, and image. It is tuned into the limitations and realities of life. It embraces many concerns and is at ease wandering through them to investigate, question, and discover. Its multidimensional and labyrinthine approach is often confusing and even necessarily, at least for a time, confused. Soul is the committed lover of art, culture, learning, music, and imagination. All of these, while grounded in and expressive of the human, are also conduits of intuition—and *intuition is the voice of the soul, while conscience is the voice of the spirit.*

In the enlivened, growing soul, intuition accesses the higher, inspirational realm of spirit. Then, through its voiceless voice, soul guides us on our journey toward healing, life meaning, destiny, and eventually wholeness.

What society has begun to discover, initially through Jung's brilliant ground-breaking efforts, is that the dualistic view of human nature—spirit and body only— *doesn't work because it isn't true.*

The Enneagram: A Guide for Soul Making

The Enneagram invites us to think more deeply about our souls. In explaining how *One becomes nine*—how from the Unity of eternity come nine kinds of people, nine *unconscious motivations* for human activity—it entices us to look at ourselves and see how we have abused our souls. By primarily focusing on the external world, we expend our energy finding quick-fix solutions that temporarily ease the tension of life but never deal with the issue of meaning or the why of our existence.

The main body of this chapter is dedicated to a brief description of the nine personality types of the Enneagram.[8] Because soul making takes place in everyday life, we identify for each of these nine patterns the day-to-day illusions that prevent us from waking up and becoming conscious. Clearly identifying these illusions may create the tension we need to reevaluate our way of living and pursue the hard work of soul making.

First, through the Enneagram, we recognize how we have created a distortion or imbalance in our lives by compulsively overusing our strengths in self-serving ways. Until we take responsibility for the whole of our life—the positive and the negative, the wounding and the healing—we'll remain blind to the reality that there are definite consequences of the choices we make each and every day. Owning the truth of who we are frees our imaginations to journey into the invisible world of possibilities, searching for creative solutions that can restore harmony in our lives.

---

[8]Our book *What's My Type?* presents in chapter 1 fuller, more complete descriptions of the nine personality types. However, because our understanding of these nine personality types is evolving, the descriptions presented here are fresh and different, focusing more on each pattern's motivation than on common characteristics and behavioral patterns.

One of the most difficult truths for which we must take responsibility is laid bare by the Enneagram. It is the subjective need we each have to justify our approach to life by feeling we have attained a certain illusory goal. This "good feeling" is an attempt to massage our egos and avoid having to wake up to the truth of our own selfishness and narrow-mindedness. This selfish desire to feel good creates an insatiable thirst that can never be quenched. It drives us into a desert of meaningless activity and away from the river that would carry us into the depths of our own soul—to the clear, fresh, living spring of meaning.

In other words, the Enneagram describes nine obsessive personality styles, nine compulsive ways of dealing with the world. Fraught with and sustained by illusions about who we are, what is good for us, what we need, and what our destiny is, our Enneagram compulsion or type motivates us toward destructive fantasies about life and away from true soul making.

On the journey into soul, we'll first pass through layer after layer of illusion. As we move beyond each veil of illusion, we can view the truth of who we are more clearly and objectively.

These descriptions are presented in layers. The first veil of illusion is a condensed *description* of the nine Enneagram types. The next layer is the psychological *addiction* that sustains the compulsive behavior; it is a point of view that distorts our vision of reality and impairs our ability to promote true soul making.

Beneath these layers of illusion we catch a fleeting glimpse of the *Original Wound* in childhood that impaired our ability to perceive the truth accurately. The pain of this initial wound has prevented us from recognizing who we were created to be, what we were intended to contribute to life, and how we might fulfill our mission, our destiny. Later chapters will examine more carefully the Original Wound that diminished our vision and became the genesis of compulsive self-protection.

Because the Enneagram describes the structure of every person's personality, by definition every person is one and only one of these nine types.

One: The Achiever

Ones *are* Achievers, *busy beavers are they*
Just a-workin' so hard, got no time to play
Makin' lotsa lists, then checkin' 'em twice
Starts a slow burn of anger, 'cuz that's their vice.

Wanna be nice, wanna be good—
But sayin' yes to everyone gives 'em too many shoulds
Too many projects only half done
Life is hard and then you die—man, that's no fun.[9]

Achievers are active, energetic people. Tending to be self-starters, they are attracted to the role of pioneer. Often they are on the cutting edge of a movement to reform a situation in their personal or professional lives.

---

[9]From "The Enneagram Rap" by Kathleen V. Hurley, copyright © 1992 Enneagram Resources, Inc. (12262 W. New Mexico Ave., Lakewood, CO 80228). Verses from "The Enneagram Rap" will be quoted before descriptions of each of the patterns throughout this chapter. A recorded version is available from Enneagram Resources, Inc.

They keep a tight rein on their emotions, attempting to attain the perfectly balanced response. Internally critical, they often report that a mental voice points out faults and mistakes of themselves and others. They are compulsive list makers—primarily for themselves, but neither is it unheard of for a spouse, child, or co-worker of an Achiever to have a to-do list handed to him or her at the beginning of a day or, even more frustratingly, at the beginning of a weekend.

Achievers are two-speed people: stop and go. Mostly on the go, they feel guilty for being "free-loaders" if they take time for themselves. Because they struggle with feelings of being unimportant, they feel the need to rationalize their existence by working hard. Consequently, they work long hours, often at a slow and steady pace, to become good in their own eyes, by their own perfectionistic standards. Though they never reach it, what drives them is their desire to achieve perfection. Because others do not share their standards, their fail-safe method of obtaining perfection is to take control of the situation.

Before attempting something new—anything from trimming a bush to entering a new career—they're apt to read up on the topic to be certain they will do it right. Achievers live with the tension of both wanting time alone and needing relationships with others to ease their gnawing feeling of worthlessness and insecurity. Spending time in nature provides the greatest release for this tension, because it brings a sense of peace and helps them to break the myopic trap of concentrating on the task right in front of them.

Far too harsh in self-evaluation, Achievers trust compliments only if they are specific and detailed. Often they are the moral, ethical, just, honest, fair, and moderate people in a family or community. Needing to be known as "good boys" and "good girls," they will agree to do things they really don't want to do and then struggle internally with feeling taken advantage of. They would like their good qualities to shine because they are often quite ashamed of their secret internal reactions—judgmental attitudes and resentful memories.

Addiction.   The driving force behind this approach to life is an addiction to anger. Simply put, for Achievers, nothing is the way it should be. They are always dissatisfied and must work hard to improve any situation. Furthermore, because other people are not doing their share, Achievers feel left in the lurch with more than their fair allotment of responsibilities.

Achievers are rarely direct or forthright about their anger, however. Usually it rises like a slow burn, and others seldom notice their constant internal battle to contain the fire. What is apparent is their external social charm, smile, well-groomed appearance, and a slight, shy hint of their desire to be liked. Clad in emotional armor, they move through life at a steady pace, plugging away at cleaning up the battlefields others have left in disarray.

They appear to be independent, capable of handling life, and unexpressive of their own needs. Thus, Achievers take their responsible approach to life for granted, while others can take advantage of them. If only the squeaky wheel gets the oil, know that Achievers squeak only in isolated silence.

Achievers' vision has been impaired so that they see only perfection as acceptable. They see beauty only in completion and rarely in the gangling stages of growth. The only antidote for them is patience—the ability to see beyond what is and perceive the still unfolding wonder and mystery of what might be.

Original Wound.   The attitudes of compulsive Achievers camouflage their Original Wound. Blinded by an inability to trust the promises of others, Achievers can only rely on the quality and intensity of their own response to life. Sadly, painfully, they have learned not to rely on others or on life to care about or support them. Though somewhere in their early life history is an experience of not being able to trust their own understanding of the world and the people around them, they were also assigned responsibility for things over which they had no control—a recipe for persistent guilt.

Achievers compensate for the loss of trust by focusing on the present moment, to the point of becoming myopic. They lock in on the situation in which they are currently engaged and intensify their efforts. You can't learn to trust others when the quality of your own response is the determining factor in your estimation of yourself as a person. This attitude protects Achievers from the pain of their Original Wound, the pain of betrayal.

Two: The Helper

Twos *are the* Helpers, *called "livin' saints"*
But you'd better be grateful or saints they ain't
Gentle and carin' 'bout the problems you face
They're like heaven-sent angels just showerin' grace.

Give lots of advice, have answers for you
Never talk about themselves, that's strictly taboo
Bein' oh so sweet, oh so nice
Hides pride—'cuz that's their particular vice.

Helpers are centered in the emotional life, especially in their sensitivity to the feelings and personal needs of the people around them. Conversely, their own inner emotional life is arid and dull. They focus their relational sensitivity outward and thus are known as caring, considerate, kind, gentle, and helpful.

Their source of energy and personal self-worth is centered in the outer world. Therefore, it's imperative that they become proficient in the subtle art of generously responding to the needs of other people. Simultaneously, however, they're creating deeper needs in others that only Helpers can fill. They vicariously devour the emotions, pain, joy, struggle, and victory of the real life experiences of other people, for their own internal terrain lies fallow and unproductive.

Helpers' gentle, sensitive personalities act like magnets, drawing others into a warm, safe atmosphere. In the presence of Helpers other people feel free to be open, honest, and vulnerable. In turn, Helpers experience an inner warmth in these relationships that vanishes when they are alone. Alone, a vague sense of meaninglessness begins to rise up and steal their energy, so that time spent by themselves is often spent thinking of others. Because they have little interest in pursuing solitary activities, at the slightest indication that someone would appreciate their company or assistance, they will drop everything to respond. The ensuing expressions of gratitude and appreciation will, at least temporarily, ease the Helpers' constant internal loneliness.

Understandably, Helpers are often drawn to a helping profession where their focus on people can be put to good use. Although Helpers do create dependency in other people, they themselves are totally dependent upon others for their personal sense of well-being and worth. Thus, they are externally competent and internally dependent.

Blind to the dark side of their motivation, they narrowly focus on the results of their helping and allow the warmth of their personalities to determine their present and future. By concentrating on the interpersonal realm so intensely, they allow their personal lives to become disorganized, responsibilities to be ignored, and many personal projects only partially completed or left undone altogether.

Addiction. The driving force behind this approach to life is an addiction to pride. Simply put, Helpers know you need them but remain totally unconscious of their need for you. Focused completely outside themselves, they respond to situations in which they can be care givers but don't know what to do when someone offers a mutual relationship. One-way intimacy is the name of their game.

Helpers subtly engage the assistance of others in this subterfuge by massaging their egos with interest, warmth, and sensitive response. By their flattery of people, by their gentle demeanor, and by their welcoming attitude, they focus the spotlight on others. Helpers easily create an aura of confident well-being that blinds others to their subtle superiority.

Helpers tend to resent a person who refuses their help or who attempts to establish a reciprocal relationship. Taking pride in their virtuous, self-sacrificial attitude toward life, they wonder why so few people are other-centered and conclude that most people simply are selfish. Similarly, they make pride appear to be humility as they downplay their own needs and place themselves at the service of others. Their pride peeks out in their responses to unappreciative people: criticism or hurt feelings.

They can't see that their desperate desire to feel needed and appreciated by others is simply a socially acceptable but mechanical way of avoiding the pain of consciousness. Only when they turn their compassion, warmth, and sensitivity toward themselves will the lonely void of personal neediness be filled. Responding to their own needs for identity, self-worth, and intimacy will give birth to the antidote for this addiction: humility, the ability to see oneself as both needy and helpful, as both weak and strong.

Original Wound. The attitudes of compulsive Helpers camouflage their Original Wound. Blinded by an inability to trust their own dignity and goodness, Helpers have no safe place to concentrate their energy except on the world around them in the hope of finding out who they are. Sadly, painfully, they learned to invalidate and repress not only their own needs but their very dignity and personhood. Somewhere in their early life history is an experience of internal mistrust of their own feelings and needs as forms of self-indulgence that were unreliable. Thus, they focus on the eyes of others, endlessly searching for a reflection of their own face, their own identity.

Helpers compensate for the loss of trust by focusing on the present moment, even to the point of losing perspective. They lock in on the situation in which they are presently engaged and intensify their concern and desire to respond. You can't learn to trust yourself when the grateful responses that others give you become the determining factor in your estimation of yourself as a person. This attitude protects Helpers from the pain of their Original Wound, the pain of betrayal.

Three: The Succeeder

Places to go and people to see
That's the way a Three *is bound to* Succeed
Keep a smile on their face, their head in the air
So everyone'll think they're really goin' somewhere.

> *If they fail you can't tell by lookin' in their eyes*
> *Too afraid to show it, they wear a disguise*
> *Lookin', actin', dressin' like a VIP*
> *Don't matter how they feel, just what you see.*

Succeeders are smooth, political people. Hyper-aware of the feelings and needs of others, they use these perceptive capabilities to lure others into enthusiastically supporting any project or goal that will enhance their own image of confidence, competence, and capability.

Underneath their self-assured exterior lies a volcano of emotion. Succeeders are passionate about life and have deep feelings about many things. However, they are extremely controlled and cautious about revealing their feelings or thoughts in the presence of other people. They believe that any self-revelation would be political suicide in the work world, and they have learned in their personal relationships that others are incapable of handling the intensity of their emotion. They believe that it's only safe to deal with emotions in private. The loneliness that results is easier to deal with than the complicated messiness of intimacy.

Succeeders use humor outwardly and superhuman effort inwardly to regulate their emotional pressure valve. They guard themselves carefully, certain that any sign of vulnerability will be used against them. They express their anxiety by keeping relationships on the surface and moving quickly from one project or idea to another, so the response "We'll talk about that later" really means the subject is closed. Succeeders seek out relationships that are relaxing, fun, and undemanding. If a relationship becomes too demanding, negative, or energy depleting, Succeeders simply walk away—physically, emotionally, or both.

These hardworking, aggressive go-getters measure their success by the degree of admiration expressed by other people. Succeeders have a selective memory that recalls only successes, never failures. If their success depends on compromising personal values and standards, they easily find a rationale for doing so. When faced with failure, they can walk away and never look back; their loyalties vanish.

Succeeders, who tend to relate personably—but not personally—to people and to life, set no boundaries between their personal and public lives. They are professionals on twenty-four-hour call, parents who are using every opportunity to teach their children what they will need in daily life, people who identify so much with their role that they have a difficulty just being themselves. Optimistic, productive, future- and goal-oriented, they tend to think everything will work out fine, and if it doesn't, it probably wasn't good to begin with.

Addiction.   The driving force behind this approach to life is an addiction to deceit. Simply put, Succeeders think that their external image is reality. Appearance—how they look, produce, perform—is the only thing that counts. Thoughts, feelings, and personal values are private and therefore insignificant. If you expose your private life, you'll never get ahead or convince anyone you're worth anything.

Succeeders live in two worlds simultaneously, one in the spotlight at center stage, and the other on a secret island of isolation where feelings hide behind masks, failures hide behind successes, and vulnerability hides behind competency. Too shrewd to tell an outright lie, they simply won't reveal anything unless it will ultimately lead to their advantage. Any doubt on this score and they take the prudent path of silence.

Succeeders' vision has become so clouded that they are unable to distinguish between real life and playacting, truth and deception. They believe the only way to validate their existence is by becoming the best in what they do. Unless they achieve success, they feel worthless. Only through the antidote for this addiction, integrity—firmly adhering to a code of values internally and externally—will they discover what has been hidden to them: the honor, dignity, and value of their own personhood.

Original Wound. The attitudes of compulsive Succeeders camouflage their Original Wound. Disoriented by an inability to believe in the constancy of love, they search for a dependable substitute and find it in the eyes of other people who admire their success. Because admiration replaces love, they need it desperately, and no price seems too great to pay. Even when admiration is no longer an issue, they find it difficult to love themselves; that's why they can push themselves so hard to work and perform.

Succeeders compensate for the loss of love by focusing on the future, setting new goals that will continue to generate enough applause and recognition to fill the abyss of longing within. Constantly they look to the future, concentrating on potential opportunities for success. You can't learn the truth of what love is when your wrong understanding leads you to believe your drive, vision, and success are the determining factor in your estimation of yourself as a person. This attitude protects Succeeders from the pain of their Original Wound, the pain of emotional alienation.

Four: The Individualist

Individualists *are special, their number is* Four
Gushy feelings so intense they just drip on the floor
Very creative, and they love to preen
Singin' "Nobody knows the trouble I've seen."

French cuisine, the artsy scene are simple pleasures
But a friend who understands is a priceless treasure
Green with envy and actin' superior
They're feelin' unlovable, mostly inferior.

Individualists are centered in their emotional life, which they experience as an intense, private world that no one else could understand. These are deeply feeling people for whom strong passions are the essence of real living. Personal sensitivity and a keen desire for intimacy lead to a desire to be included and invited into groups, and to include others in their groups. They experience emotional extremes that range from the high lilting pitch of the emotional scale to the heavy timbre of the low, dark, and somber.

This exaggerated emphasis on feelings is given expression through their dramatic style of response and interaction. They have an exceptional ability to perceive the beauty and wonder of people and nature. This perceptive gift suddenly becomes distorted whenever they compare themselves to the perceived beauty in others and judge themselves lacking and therefore inferior.

Insecurity engulfs them when their feelings of being inferior collide with their intense need for intimate relationships. Fearing they will be rejected or abandoned for someone more interesting or appealing, they cling too tightly and become possessive. Their fear then becomes a self-fulfilling prophecy. The sense of loss and loneliness that ensues causes them to re-create and mull over every moment, not just of that experience but of their entire history of disappointments with people.

They analyze and reanalyze the past in an attempt to understand and resolve the pain they carry. They believe that to understand and be understood by even one person is the key that would open the door to real life. Like E.T., they need to find home—a place where they no longer need to be self-protective, but can be themselves in an atmosphere of both intimacy and respect.

Lacking confidence in dealing with the world of practical things, Individualists cover their self-doubt by striving for excellence as a person—authenticity of expression, for example, and development of talents and gifts. Their emotional sensitivity runs so deep and their feelings can become so confused and difficult to sort out that they often turn to artistic expression, where symbols continue to speak to the soul long after words have been exhausted. Individualists, who can appear fragile and temperamental, are actually strong people who have much to contribute to life. They thrive on anything new and different that will give expression to the unique individuality they have always hungered for.

Addiction.   The driving force behind this approach to life is an addiction to envy. Simply put, Individualists are hyper-aware of all the good qualities and possessions of others, and not seeing their own hidden strength, want what other people have. They live with the illusion that they will not be prepared to live their real life until they have developed every possible potential and thoroughly understand themselves.

By constantly comparing themselves to others and highlighting all they can't and don't have, they allow their inner life to be dominated by an intense attitude of pessimism. This negative outlook leads them to look first at the obstacles and pitfalls in any project or life situation. By being prepared for the worst they believe that they might have a chance to circumvent the inevitable difficulties. If they always prepare for the worst, they protect themselves from unexpected disappointments.

Gripped by a dread that they will not become the person they were created to be, they feel ordinary and useless; they are driven to understand themselves in an effort to discover a meaning and purpose to which they can dedicate their lives. Feelings of being inferior plague them, and they fear that if they disappeared today there would be little evidence they had existed.

Individualists see themselves as so ordinary and plain that all they can feel is envy and longing for everything they recognize in others. The only antidote that will neutralize the unbridled forces of their emotions is serenity— the composure, steadiness, and self-control needed to put focused energy and hard work into expressing their gifts and talents.

Original Wound.   The attitudes of compulsive Individualists camouflage their Original Wound. Crippled by an inability to hope in others, Individualists of necessity can only risk placing all their hope in themselves. Unable to trust others because their experience gives them reason to expect abandonment, they feel intense grief and anguish. Somewhere in their early life history there was an experience of physical or emotional desertion that devastated their self-perception to the core; thus, they blame themselves for being too ordinary.

Individualists compensate for the loss of hope by concentrating on the past in a desperate search to understand exactly why they were rejected, even though this search makes them pessimistic. Only by focusing on what happened and why do they believe they'll be able to improve and become a lovable and desirable person. You don't need to risk hoping in others if you concentrate your efforts on yourself and on things that have already taken place. This attitude protects Individualists from the pain of their Original Wound, the pain of abandonment.

Five: The Observer

Fives are Observers—eccentric old birds
Gather lots of knowledge, don't need to be heard
Sit and plan and ponder and think things through
Till all the time is gone—there's no time to do.

Stop feelin' and emotin' and reactin'—my god!
It's the only way to keep your feet on the sod
Interestin' people and clever for sure
Who find social climbin' just pure manure.

Observers are reserved people who strive for an objective, dispassionate perspective. Their first love is knowledge and information, and their great desire is to be able to distill knowledge into wisdom. For this task they need time—time alone to think, ponder, and reflect.

Observers learned early in life how to set the boundaries that would ensure their privacy. No matter where they live, they find a quiet place, claim it as their own, and retreat there as much as possible. Although Observers often come across as loners who resent intrusion, frequently they secretly feel lonely and hope that someone involved in life and interesting to be with will show up on their doorstep for a brief, casual visit. However, they would rarely, if ever, initiate such an encounter, dreading the possible embarrassment of being treated as an intrusion.

Their passion for objectivity demands detachment. Though Observers feel deeply about much of life, they intentionally isolate their feelings so they won't interfere with logical evaluation of a person or situation. Thus, they tend to ignore relational and emotional issues when trying to solve problems, or in living life in general. No matter how much they have learned about life, they never feel quite ready for or capable of taking on the responsibility of direct involvement or commitment.

Observers' strength lies in their ability to perceive and comprehend life on a broad scale. They quickly sift out feelings from facts and then pierce through to the core of the issue to summarize life, people, and situations with a dispassionate logic that's often as tactless as it is accurate. Because of their emotional detachment they excel at delegation, mediation, and research. Also, they love adventures—vacations to interesting places, skulking in the nooks and crannies of out-of-the-way destinations, discovering new paths of knowledge or understanding—for these are opportunities to learn and add to their storehouse of little-known, extraordinary information.

Observers are often witty, charming, and attractive people who are the last to know that they are likable. Their nonconforming attitudes and unusual insights into life make them clever and interesting conversationalists. They love to perpetuate their unorthodox, eccentric image, and they use it to excuse themselves from developing social skills or becoming involved in life.

Addiction.   The driving force behind this approach to life is an addiction to greed. Simply put, Observers want to use their energy gathering observations, becoming wise, and protecting their privacy. They feel inadequate as human beings and believe that a wealth of uncommon knowledge, time alone, and original insights will make up for their deficiencies. They live with the illusion that knowing about life is the same as living it.

In conversation they primarily listen, allowing others to take the initiative while they remain silent. Then, toward the end of the conversation, they will speak, summarizing the topic with the coolness of a philosophy professor teaching the basics of logic. They want to be known as wise. Their slightly superior manner is not only intimidating to others but also irritating.

Being slow to make commitments, Observers will normally respond to any request with one of two responses: no or maybe. No preserves their privacy, and maybe gives them time to think and decide whether they want to fit this activity into their schedule.

Observers are plagued with memories of being shunned or seen as offensive for saying something with the intention of being helpful that others heard as insensitive, rigid, or superior. Thus, an underlying uneasy or awkward feeling permeates their personal relationships. Believing that the only safe course to steer is into the private world of knowledge, information, and logical analysis prevents them from developing the antidote for their addiction, generosity. Through generosity they would relinquish part of what they love the most—time, privacy, and knowledge—but they would, in return, reap the benefits of relating to and improving the community.

Original Wound. The attitudes of compulsive Observers camouflage their Original Wound. Crippled by an inability to hope in themselves as persons, Observers of necessity only dare to hope in the external, impersonal world of knowledge. Their experience—like a deep, slashing knife of sorrow—gave them reason to expect abandonment. Somewhere in their early life history is an experience of physical or emotional desertion that devastated their self-perception to the core, leaving them feeling personally hopeless.

Observers compensate for the loss of hope by concentrating on the past, trying to understand where and how they fit into life. They dwell on knowledge they have already gained, distilling it into wisdom, and on experiences in the past, which they try to understand by objective analysis. You do not need to risk hoping in yourself if your knowledge about things that have already taken place becomes the determining factor in your estimation of yourself as a person. This attitude protects Observers from the pain of their Original Wound, the pain of abandonment.

Six: The Guardian

Sixes *are* Guardians, *responsible for sure*
Followin' the rules is the way they feel secure
Active, charming people and oh so gracious
But if you dare to cross them their behavior's outrageous.

Keepers of tradition, they trust the tried and true
Why change what works for something cheap and new?
'Cuz decisions are so difficult, often very scary
They'll seek advice from everyone—fear makes them wary.

Guardians are information-oriented people who take their responsibilities very seriously. An underlying sense of insecurity and a desire to be included leads to their often exaggerated need for reassurance and personal contact.

Guardians, the most naturally domestic of all types, often become the information hub and gathering point of the community they most value. When their primary group is the family—and often it is—good, solid values will permeate everything from child rearing to family celebrations. If they commit themselves to another kind of community—a stable institution or a professional organization, for example—the customs, norms, and rules of the group will provide the Guardians' grounding.

Caution permeates their personality and lifestyle, for they will never jeopardize themselves or those they love through reckless action or careless thinking. Guardians dedicate themselves to upholding and passing on sound moral values, for they know these are the basic foundations for a strong, healthy society. By handling their own insecurities through defining morality in a rigid way, however, they become opinionated and unforgiving of all who hold different values.

On the lighter side, laughter and fun will be the highlight of the day or week as a needed release from their energetic and hardworking daily routine. Graciousness will permeate their everyday demeanor—unless they are crossed—and will be their hallmark in social situations.

When they are crossed, a backbone of steel, whose origin is anger at not feeling accepted or respected, will make them stubborn, tough negotiators, but only in that particular situation. Then their need to know they are doing well and are liked by others takes over, and they return to their normal style of personal interaction and dialogue. Theirs is the path of duty and dedication. They prefer keeping to tradition—in family, church, and society—because they trust what has been proven to work and fear the risk involved in attempting anything new.

Addiction.   The driving force behind this approach to life is an addiction to fear. Simply put, Guardians live with a low-level anxiety about life, a vague apprehension that leaves them wary, cautious, and feeling incapable. To their way of thinking, however, fear is prudence, and it makes a person seek out the information needed to make appropriate decisions. They live with the illusion that although life is dangerous, they can make it safe with thorough preparation and a responsible attitude.

Guardians are always inquiring—either directly or indirectly—about what's currently going on in the lives of everyone they know. Keeping abreast of personal information about other people helps them to feel connected and alleviates their fear of being left out and unsure where they fit in life. Remaining active eases their anxiety because it eliminates free time, which would allow all their worries to rise. Being accepted by a group soothes their greatest worry—that they have nowhere they belong.

Constant and tangible signs of reassurance give them a sense of confidence that they are doing well, that they are liked, and that they are welcome. Without this reassurance, their anxiety can grow to the point that they become overfearful about possible or imagined threats to their security. Uncomfortable with new experiences, they will always choose to remain in their familiar surroundings or keep postponing a new experience until a later date.

They need to feel safe because they feel caught in perpetual aloneness. Never being certain if they're important enough to be remembered or included gives rise in them to great insecurity and fear. Constant connecting is Guardians' way of reminding others that they do care about them and want to be a part of their lives. The only antidote that will neutralize their addiction to fear is courage. It demands courage for them to halt the frenzy of activity and constant connecting and create open spaces of time for quiet reflection. In the silence they can face their fears and find the peace of being at home within themselves.

Original Wound.   The attitudes of compulsive Guardians camouflage their Original Wound. Crippled by an inability to trust other people or themselves, Guardians continually seek to have their inner ideas and plans corroborated by others. Yet, no amount of shoring up is ever enough, because their experience has given them reason to reject the reliability of information they receive from others or from within. Somewhere in their early life history they experienced their own feelings and responses to life as untrustworthy and couldn't fully count on what others said or did. Thus, they are on an endless search to find the confidence, stability, and security that were lost.

Guardians compensate for the loss of trust by focusing on the present moment, even to the point of becoming overresponsible. They pour their energy into the people and the situations with which they are currently engaged, needing once again to be assured that they are adequate people. You don't need to trust others or yourself if your own sense of responsibility reaffirms your value to others and becomes the determining factor in your estimation of yourself as a person. This attitude protects Guardians from the pain of their Original Wound, the pain of betrayal.

Seven: The Dreamer

Sevens *are* Dreamers, *visionary schemers*
Fancy lotsa money and drivin' new Beemers
Optimistic and happy, find it tough growin' up
'Cuz they shirk from work and run to fun and follow
    Lady Luck.

So mentally creative, with genius unmatched
Don't try to pen them up 'cuz they'll break the latch
Friends are a joy—just livin' feels like heaven
They'll be your friend until the end with happiness their
    leaven.

Dreamers are optimistic, happy, and fun-loving people—compulsively so. They don't look at the negative side of life. Theirs is an easy optimism that will not admit of problems that can't be solved or of situations that can't be fixed. They like to spend time remembering the good things in their lives and want others to see them as positively as they see themselves.

Their minds race at a hundred miles an hour with ideas and plans to make life easier and better. They develop highly analytical minds and are drawn to people and situations that can stimulate them intellectually. Their difficulty comes in putting their ideas into action or following through on their plans, especially in their personal lives. Because they feel incapable of handling life, they tend to procrastinate and not bring stressful situations to closure. Unable to read the motives of others, they tend to presume the best of everyone and therefore are gullible. They mask their feelings of incapability with social charm and good cheer.

Dreamers take great pleasure in pleasing others and making them happy. Their deep love for family and friends is evidenced in their lifelong loyalty. Because they have difficulty expressing emotion directly, they constantly try to show others how much they care by doing small kind and thoughtful things. This is part of the secret serious side of Dreamers that many people either miss altogether or simply take for granted. Dreamers are always delighted when someone acknowledges and values their thoughtfulness because it means they've conveyed their intended message.

Feeling unable to handle life's more serious issues, they use humor to deflect tension and to disguise any of their own negative feelings. Dreamers resent and will even aggressively reject the expectations of others. On the other hand, these "free spirits" feel comfortable with and even excited by life's challenges and display great energy and enthusiasm in overcoming them.

Dreamers love to get others involved in their plans and activities. They have a preference for team responsibility and group decision making. They are the kind of people others like to have around because they bring a lightness of spirit and happiness wherever they go.

Addiction. The driving force behind this approach to life is an addiction to gluttony. Simply put, Dreamers want more and more of whatever makes them happy— not necessarily food and drink, though these may also be attractions, but any activity that gives them life and vitality. They live with the illusion that all pain and sorrow in life can be eliminated by thinking positively and doing only those things that make you feel good.

They are jacks-of-all-trades, whose lack of staying power can make them masters of none. Because they have a hard time growing up and "getting their act together," they live off the luxury of the happiness they create in life with their humor, charm, and scintillating minds.

Dreamers' tendency toward lighthearted relationships diverts attention from their depth of character, and they can appear shallow. They would rather that you and they focus together on experiencing the positive side of life. Their attitude is, There's nothing you can't enjoy if you just put your mind to it!

Dreamers, who find the complexity of life over-whelming, are faced with the difficult task of balancing their idealism with a large dose of hard work and practical realism. The only antidote that will enable them to generate true happiness in their own lives and in the lives of others is fortitude, the ability to endure the frustrations that come with stage-by-stage growth. Fortitude provides them with self-discipline and the power to deal with the whole of life by applying their well-developed minds to personal and communal problems and to carrying out creative solutions.

Original Wound. The attitudes of compulsive Dreamers camouflage their Original Wound. Crippled by an inability to love others, Dreamers of necessity must take care of themselves first. They are afraid to love others because their experience has given them reason to expect to be disconnected from the people they love. Somewhere in their early life history is an experience of emotional severance that caused them to shut down their emotions, especially the ability to love others.

Dreamers compensate for the loss of love by concentrating on the future, because it distances them from other people. They dwell on possibilities, ideas, and plans that will make their world happier and better. You don't need to risk loving others if your ideas and optimism about the future become the determining factors in your estimation of yourself as a person. This attitude protects Dreamers from the pain of their Original Wound, the pain of emotional alienation.

Eight: The Confronter

Eights *are* Confronters—*they know the power of words*
You may regret you met, but not forget you heard
Ambitious and creative, lustin' after power
They think they're right—they stand and fight until you
    cower.

Tenderness lies hidden like a mountain's vein of gold
Sparkles in their carin' for the young, the weak, the old
Justice is their purpose, but their strength makes people
    nervous
Only God is unafraid to lead them into service.

Confronters are powerful people. Concentrating on their
own abilities to make things happen, they are blunt and
firm, full of life, strength, and energy that they splash
spontaneously all over the world. They like being thought
of as determined and original people who would never
unthinkingly follow the crowd or live a life of apathy.
Some are loud and raucous, others are reserved and proper,
but all are direct in communication.

Justice is their issue, first for themselves and then for
others. Having clearly defined ideas regarding what is just
makes them extremely aware of how others use people
and situations to serve themselves. What they are blind to
is how they also take advantage of others to gain power.
They'll pursue their cause with relentless persistence and
in the process become champions for all the underdogs
who lack the power and strength Confronters possess.

Although Confronters exude tremendous strength, they seldom feel as strong and secure as they appear.

Members of their own family and anyone they classify as oppressed—for example, children, the sick, or the elderly—tap into Confronters' own unconscious feelings of vulnerability. Thus, the tenderness hidden deep within them comes forth as a fierce protectiveness and determination to act on these others' behalf. Although expressive of their deep caring for these people both in word and action, Confronters remain emotionally distant.

Generally, Confronters are emotionally insensitive to themselves and others. Because they don't understand sensitivity, they mistake it for weakness or indecisiveness and respond with disdain, anger, or disgust. They express love for others by doing something rather than verbally expressing their feelings, and they prefer to have other people express care for them in practical ways also.

Dedication to and concern for family will lead Confronters who are parents to prepare their children for the harsh realities of the world. In general, then, children will be taught how to overcome difficulties by themselves, learning to stand on their own two feet and fend for themselves.

Addiction.   The driving force behind this approach to life is an addiction to lust. Simply put, Confronters have a ravenous appetite for life and experience, and they intend to satisfy their passions through power and control. Easily bored by routine and possessing an overabundance of energy, they doggedly maneuver through obstacles until they reach positions of power. They live with the illusion that life is about having influence and making things happen; thus, they never let down their guard and are always planning the next several moves needed to get ahead.

They feel everything depends on them and that they need to light a fire under others to get things moving. For them, life is always going too slowly. They like involvement and being on the go. They love stimulation.

Unconcerned—or at least undeterred—by what other people think or say, Confronters have no fear of expressing themselves. They are able to handle pressure and stress and so deal well with crises. Experience has taught them to trust their abilities to be quick, thorough, and creative in any situation—even the unexpected. The self-confidence that has grown from awareness of their own capability is often interpreted as arrogance because it lacks sensitivity.

They need to feel strong because they are held fast by an internal experience of weakness that they struggle to overcome. Their strength—a wonderful and much-needed gift in society—needs to be tempered with vulnerability and understanding. The only antidote that will neutralize their addiction to lust is compassion, which balances their power to act with the power of empathy and gentleness.

Original Wound. The attitudes of compulsive Confronters camouflage their Original Wound. Crippled by an inability to love themselves, Confronters focus on the external world as they bury their emotional needs. They are unable to love themselves because their experience has given them reason to expect the people they love will be insensitive to their emotional needs. Somewhere in their early life history is an experience of unfilled emotional need that caused them to minimize their emotions and maximize their power to control life.

Confronters compensate for the loss of love by concentrating on the future, even though doing so causes them to work from hidden motives. They dwell on intensifying their own response to life and getting their own way. You don't need to risk loving yourself if the intensity of your strength and your passion for life become the determining factors in your estimation of yourself as a person. This attitude protects Confronters from the pain of their Original Wound, the pain of emotional alienation.

Nine: The Preservationist

Nines *are* Preservationists, *peace is all they seek*
Will sit and watch the mountains grow for hours, days,
and weeks
At work they're respected, but emotionally neglected
So bein' easygoing is how they stay connected.

Wanna argue? Better plan to be alone
'Cuz, man, they're outta here, and you are on your own
No settin' goals or workin' or ever makin' hay
These gentle, lazy people always choose to play.

Preservationists are easygoing people who prize peace so highly that they hold their personal relationships at bay through the power of their silence. Simply refusing to argue, they'll leave the room—either emotionally or physically—rather than enter into any confrontation. Others can think what they like, say what they think, feel what they want, and Preservationists will do what they please. If they give in to the pressure of the moment, they know they'll resent it later.

These are power-oriented people who use power in a quiet way. Generally affable and pleasant, they are also fiercely independent, privately clinging to their own ideas with stubborn tenacity.

Preservationists have a profound connection to the earth. Feeling at home and unthreatened in nature, they find that time outdoors restores the grounding that slips away in the activities and pressures of everyday life. Thus, they will always be attracted to outdoor pursuits because these reconnect them to their roots and give them the peace they long for.

Professionally and socially respected, Preservationists protect and enhance their reputation whenever possible. What others think of them is important because they think so little of themselves. Thus, in their public and private lives they can look like two different people. In the world all their best qualities shine; at home or in the world of personal feelings and needs, they will usually take the easy way out.

Preservationists intentionally keep a low profile so as not to become a target for others' aggression or attention.

They say little about themselves unless asked a direct question, avoid even friendly heated discussions, keep their opinions to themselves, and overall take care of themselves better than any other type.

Addiction.   The driving force behind this approach to life is an addiction to laziness. Simply put, Preservationists use their tremendous strength to preserve the status quo rather than to accomplish goals. They ward off outside opposition with passive power. They interpret their laziness in the personal realm as humble acceptance. After all, in time everything passes, so why get upset about things you can't change? They live with the illusion that professionally and socially they can do whatever is required, but in their private life physical presence alone should be sufficient.

Preservationists often have a place in their home—a chair, a room, a workshop, or a secluded spot in the yard—where they can generally be found. Withdrawing to this sanctuary, they think, read, relax, or enjoy their hobbies.

They also resist inner work. With an easygoing mask and lighthearted humor they slough off any activity that requires an examination of their own feelings. Theirs is a deep undercurrent of past resentment and pain, and they fear that internal development might force them to face issues and cause turmoil and tension they won't have the strength to handle.

They need to feel peaceful because they feel caught in continual distress, which they therefore want to avoid at all costs. There are times when lighthearted humor in the midst of a stressful situation is the necessary element to release intense pressure; preservationists, however, consistently use this affable quality to escape having to deal with reality in their personal life. The only antidote that will neutralize their addiction to laziness in their personal life is diligence—the vigorous and persistent effort needed to commit themselves to intimate, life-giving relationships and to work toward accomplishing personal life goals.

Original Wound.   The attitudes of compulsive Preservationists camouflage their Original Wound. Crippled by an inability to hope in others or themselves, Preservationists of necessity search for reliability in a balance of inner stamina and outer tranquillity. Only when they feel they have control over both their inner and outer worlds do they feel safe. Their experience has given them reason to believe they are not important enough that anyone—not even they themselves—should care about them. Somewhere in their early life history is an experience of physical or emotional desertion that made them devalue themselves as persons. Thus, they are on an endless search to find the grounding for their existence, which they have identified as peace.

Preservationists compensate for the loss of hope by focusing on the past, even though doing so locks them into the hopelessness of realizing that things are unchangeable. They dwell on events in their lives that tell them they are not valuable to others and to themselves. You don't need to hope in others or in yourself if the sadness of past events becomes the determining factor in your estimation of yourself as a person. This attitude protects Preservationists from the pain of their Original Wound, the pain of abandonment.

Imagination and Intuition

The first step in soul making is seeing our Enneagram compulsion clearly in our lives and realizing it describes a state of sleepwalking. Automatic responses are not free; they come from psychologically and spiritually sleeping people. However, facing that truth causes a pain that for many people is too great to bear, and so they choose to avoid even this first step.

One of the reasons people find a reassessment of their life too painful is that they have lost the capacity for imagination and intuition, those interior functions of the soul that can open the door and point the way out. Not being able to imagine a remedy for a painful situation, many people choose not to admit it exists in the first place.

Creative imagination and intuition—two vital nutrients for the healthy growth of our own soul and the soul of the world—are dormant in most of us and need to be reawakened. These natural soul-making abilities were left behind on the playground of childhood. There we exchanged them for the realism, hard work, and cynicism that we were told would protect us in a harsh world.

Imagination gives form to intuition. An active imagination is one of the natural resources of all children. Adults can guide children to use their imaginations in creative, life-enhancing ways. They don't, however, possess the power to permit or prevent children from having and using imagination. In fact, adults don't even possess the power to prevent themselves from having and using imagination.

In the young and the old, both consciously and unconsciously, imagination bubbles forth like a life-giving spring in a desert of daily routines. We use our imaginations when we dream about how life would be if we won the lottery, how to talk with someone who has argued with us, how to improve a valued relationship, how to solve a problem, how to get ahead in our job, or where we might go on our summer vacation. The choice, then, is not whether we'll have or not have an imagination, but whether we'll choose to use our imagination in positive or negative ways.

Could it be that children whose free and natural imaginations are encouraged to develop will always be in touch with their intuitions, be aware of possibilities, and be in touch with their inner selves? Similarly, will children in whom imagination is subverted or discouraged lose their intuitions and imaginations—Can you lose integral parts of yourself?—or will they express these aptitudes in darker ways?

When positive, the creative meanderings of the imagination into the world of soul ignite the intuitive spark of possibility. This intuition must then be tested in the outer world of reality to see whether or not it contains truth. If not, the inquisitiveness of the soul continues to search out further possibilities until, at last, a truth that was previously hidden in the invisible world becomes a visible reality. In this process there are many more failures than successes. But if we learn from our failures, we'll grow in wisdom.

I (Ted) remember as a child of three I had a clear intuition about what I was to do with my life. I vividly remember where I was and that I was "alone in a crowd." Too young then to know the words I needed to verbalize my intuition, I was six before I could say, "I want to understand why people do what they do."

Mostly I said it to myself, because when people asked me, "What do you want to be when you grow up?" I didn't even know there were professions that focused on such things. But as I grew older, that question was a very serious one for me to answer. Whenever an adult asked it, I tried to convey this sense of what I was supposed to do with my life that burned in my heart. The feeling went beyond a desire—it felt like a calling. Little did I realize then how much it had to do with my Enneagram number—Four.

However, that childhood intuition, which came to me from the very center of my heart, has guided my every major step in life from that moment to this one. It has led me down many unusual paths of experience and education, none of which, upon looking back, would I change, though in the experience many were embarrassing and painful. As a child I interpreted my "calling" as religious and, after high school, entered seminary. But even there, it wasn't the social position that goes along with ministry that attracted me but the desire to understand people and—something that my adult self added on to my childhood intuition—assist them in understanding themselves.

The years spent in religious ministry took me down many roads the people around me didn't understand. I investigated layer after layer in the human mind, probing the effect of childhood trauma on adult feelings and behavior, discerning spiritual experience in others and myself, and through lecturing and writing assisting people on their journeys inward into self-awareness.

After years of work in this field, it became clear that this specifically religious expression for my life was no longer working for me. In the process of resigning the clerical state, however, it became clear that I was not leaving my calling but continuing to follow it. My original call is the one I continued to honor, so that resigning the clerical state was not an abandonment of my call but a response to an inner knowing that I needed to create the freedom to pursue my call more intentionally. Consequently, I have pursued my call by becoming a pastoral counselor and spiritual director, and by dedicating myself to researching, writing, and speaking about the Ennegram and soul making.

If you were to ask me, "By following your childhood intuition, have you always been happy?" I would respond, "Of course not!" Happiness is the result of many daily decisions, and I make as many mistakes in the everyday world as the next guy. But if you were to ask, "By following your intuition, have you found meaning and purpose?" I would excitedly answer, "Yes! Of course! That's precisely it!"

Intuition and imagination connect us with ourselves deep inside. They provide a groundedness to our lives that guides us. As children we need this kind of guidance—the kind that honors our real selves, builds on our talents, and creates the kind of longing that challenges us from within to the discipline and hard work needed to mold our personalities into something useful and empowering to ourselves and to others. Whenever we respectfully honor and acknowledge our intuitions or develop our imagination, we are in the sacred world of soul making. Upon that kind of foundation, people can build a life worth living.

Or, as the saying goes, "Are you living a life worth leaving?"

Discovering a New Vision

In this book we will journey, step by step, into the depths of each personality pattern of the Enneagram. As we penetrate layers and layers of camouflage in human personality, we are exploring and expanding our souls.

Attempting to answer the questions often posed to us in seminars will lead us into the Original Wound of each pattern, both to touch and to understand its limitations and strengths. We will address the ambiguities in the Three, the Six, and the Nine—patterns that repress and prefer the same part of their soul, or center of intelligence.

Our goal is to bring the light of understanding and compassion into each layer of the nine personalities until at last we enter the wildly beautiful wounded womb of each pattern. Here, we will come to understand how the Original Wound—the unconscious source of much of life's pain—can become the greatest blessing of all both for us and for the world.

However, we have also chosen to set this book in a larger context. As the 1990s proceed, we prepare to cross the boundary of a decade, a century, and a millennium. We sense in the culture that this is not simply a passing of time but the passing of an era. In the depth of the *world soul* a new hope, vitality, and vision is arising. A new feminine consciousness is rising to unite with a new masculine consciousness, the child within every human imagination is rising to unite with an overserious adult culture, and the thirst for freedom that burns in parched throats will be quenched not only politically and economically but also spiritually.

We call this movement soul making for the twenty-first century, and the wisdom of the Enneagram is a surefooted guide to making these possibilities real. Through the self-understanding that the Enneagram initiates, inner unity is possible, community is possible, and a deep abiding awareness of the dignity and beauty of every human being becomes the foundation of transformation, healing, and renewal for the individual and the world.

For Personal or Group Work

Questions for reflection will conclude every chapter of this book. They are offered as a means of working through the issues the chapter presents. Discuss these questions and your answers to them with a friend, or write your answers in your journal.

1. Identify your Enneagram type.[10] Knowing what type you are is just the beginning, however. Until you personalize the descriptions you read—until you see *in your own life experience* how you express your Enneagram type—this knowledge will be of little use to you in the project of soul making. Choosing at least three of the qualities of your Enneagram type, try to describe various ways—from obvious to subtle—that you exhibit these qualities in daily life situations.

2. When they are properly used, the powers of the soul are turned inward, and we discover our true feelings, we learn to think for ourselves, and we learn to act with conviction that leads to freedom, unity, and true understanding. When the powers of the soul are turned outward, they become the compulsive and mechanical feelings, thoughts, and actions that compose our Enneagram type.

Look beneath the three compulsive qualities you worked with in answering the question above to discover the gifts that are their origin. These qualities point you toward soul making. Describe how you've seen these qualities emerging in your life.

For example, beneath compulsive self-pity is the gift of emotional sensitivity; therefore, a person who is full of

---

[10]If you do not already know your Enneagram number, you may want to consult the introduction and chapter 1 of our book *What's My Type?*, which goes into greater detail about how to identify your type and describes the nine patterns in greater detail.

self-pity is also emotionally sensitive to self and others. When such a person begins to tell stories of compassion for others and self, soul making takes a step forward in that person's life.

3. Everyone has imagination and intuition, although not everyone can immediately recognize these inner faculties—they may have been dormant or ignored for years. Identify an intuition that has come to you, either recently or long ago. It may have been an intuition about something that would happen in the outer world that then did happen; it may have been an intuition that someone would call you who then did call you; it may have been an intuition about something you should do in the near future; or it may have been an intuition from long ago about your destiny. Simply recognizing intuitions as such develops our intuitive life and connects us a little more deeply to our real selves.

If you identified an early intuition, does it mean anything to you today? Has the meaning of it grown or evolved from when you first recognized it? Do you often have intuitions like this one and then ignore them? If the intuition was about your personal life, what might it be telling you about yourself? Your destiny? Your purpose in life?

4. As you observe our culture and civilization, what are the indications to you that the soul of humanity is stirring? What are the contrary forces of violence and brutality that you feel most imperil the positive movements? Do you see a new era coming forth in the twenty-first century? How would you describe what you see coming?

2

Rivers of the Mind

Ever more people today have the means
to live, but no meaning to live for.
—VICTOR FRANKL

It was an incredible experience, after the passing of almost three decades, once again to be sitting at dawn on the banks of the Mississippi River. Questions and thoughts floated through the woman's mind like brilliantly colored butterfly wings as she watched the water flow with tremendous power and grace toward its final destination.

How many heart-rending, awe-inspiring secrets from the past lie buried in the mud below? Countless stories of the river—from Mark Twain's *The Adventures of Huckleberry Finn* to portrayals of romance and treachery on luxurious riverboats—have entertained generations of people. How could anyone today understand and love that historic period if not for the creative genius of vivid imaginations that, once recorded on paper, took on a life of their own?

How many more stories will forever remain untold? Real-life stories of fortunes won and lost, hopes and dreams whispered on the waters that came true; others that slowly drifted into an eternal tomb beneath the dark surface. Now the myriad tales of life and love, laughter and tears, birth and death were being transposed in her mind into the rhythmic patterns of a river song. She hummed an unfamiliar tune as the air around her vibrated with the music of romance, mystery, life. Gratefully, she felt life from the river once again soaking into the marrow of her bones. She sat perfectly still on the warm, moist earth as if waiting to be reborn.

At midday, as she sat mesmerized by sunlight dancing lightly across the broad, powerful expanse, a long forgotten memory suddenly flashed through her mind. As if it were yesterday, she could see the sun filtering through the cool, green leaves of the northern Minnesota woods to dance on a tiny trickle of clear, pure water. Smiling, she wondered if perhaps at this exact moment there might be a child triumphantly standing with one foot on either shore of the headwaters of the mighty Mississippi—just as she had straddled those shores so many years ago.

"It's remarkable," she thought, "that the tiny trickle of water I can still picture so vividly in my mind contains all the vital potential of becoming this proud old river I sit beside today."

Leaning toward the water, she whispered, "What are you trying to teach me, you wise old woman? What do I need to learn? Speak to me, speak to me."

Staring into the water, it seemed the old river woman began to move with an undulant sensuality, almost as if taunting her to be more passionate, more giving, more supple and flowing.

Sometime after the sun slipped over the horizon, she began to think about the river from its beginning till now. "You were so pure and simple in the beginning," she thought. "But as you flowed along your path, your life increased, and always, growing in the darkness beneath your bosom, was more and more life, life that you would nurture, preserve, and then offer to all who came to your shores."

"Yet," she thought, "no matter how much life the river gave away, she only became stronger, deeper, wider, more powerful."

The chill in the night air signaled that the time had come to leave. It had been a good day, and she was grateful that the powerful old river had splashed the droplets of wisdom her parched soul had been longing for. As she rose from the ground and turned away from the river, she mused, "I'm like the river. Only I began with a tiny, pure trickle from the waters of Conscious Love." As she walked toward home, the moon was bright and the air was warm, yet she could hear the faint sounds of the water slapping against the shore, encouraging her to move more deeply and freely into the flow of her own life.

The Loss of the Soul

In chapter 1, we wrote that Western civilization has not understood the proper place of the soul for many centuries. What have we lost in the banishment of the feminine soul from our individual and collective conscious understanding? The Enneagram begins to reveal answers to that question.

Because we haven't valued soul—either for the individual or for the society—we haven't valued soul making. Neither aware of nor having the tools for turning the powers of soul inward, we have turned our soul power outward in compulsive living. Chasing illusory happiness, we simultaneously give our compulsive personalities free rein and do not recognize how obsessive we've become. An addictive society is the result.[1]

Remembering that when it comes to the interior life, spirit is expressive of the masculine approach and soul of the feminine, we can say that, on another level, loss of soul has deprived us of conscious understanding of the feminine values of life. Therefore, not only have feminine values and qualities remained immature, but they have been distorted in both their individual and their collective expressions.

Masculine and feminine values, together and in balance, yield complementary benefits that enrich life. When either overwhelms the other, neither is life-giving. In our society—deprived of soul and therefore of a conscious understanding of the feminine—we've been looking at

---

[1]There are several important recent books on this topic: for example, Marion Woodman's *The Owl Was a Baker's Daughter* (Toronto: Inner City Books, 1980) and *Addiction to Perfection* (Toronto: Inner City Books, 1982); *When Society Becomes an Addict,* by Anne Wilson Schaef, Ph.D. (San Francisco: Harper & Row, 1987); and *Addiction and Grace,* by Gerald G. May, M.D. (San Francisco: Harper & Row, 1988).

the feminine through the wrong lens, the lens of masculine understanding. However, just as masculine values were never intended to be evaluated through a feminine perspective, feminine values can't be understood from a masculine viewpoint.

Suppose you and your neighbor both realized you needed new eyeglasses. Would you simply exchange your glasses so that each of you could have a new pair, or would you go to your eye doctor for a new prescription? Of course, exchanging glasses would be absurd. By exchanging glasses not only could you damage your vision, you would also distort your perception of the world around you!

And that's precisely the point. But unfortunately, the feminine lenses—the eyeglasses that perceive the feminine without distortion—were shattered long ago.[2] Ever since, we have all been using the same pair of glasses—the same masculine prescription—to evaluate everything and everyone. Doing so has created a distorted perception of *both* masculine and feminine values, strengths, gifts, and talents.

In this distortion the value of masculine qualities has been exaggerated; we have viewed them as if through a magnifying glass. The value of feminine qualities has all but disappeared under a reducing glass. The world needs new, accurate eyeglasses—a new vision of both masculine and feminine.

---

[2]See chapter 1, under Soul Making, for the history of this destruction.

Naming the qualities and gifts that were lost when the feminine soul was officially discarded is not easy, because it has been so long since they faded from clear view. Even as we name them we are aware that our list is incomplete and our vision is fuzzy. A clear understanding of these qualities is only beginning to emerge as we play out the last act of the great human drama heralding the birth of the twenty-first century.

The healthy strength of the feminine carries respect for experience, emotion, feeling, personal knowledge, interconnecting, equality, partnership, understanding of relationship and intimacy, personal and collective validation of history or myth, images, imagination, humor, the freedom to question and investigate, and consciousness. True feminine understanding connects us to and reveals to us the Divine Feminine in all creation.

All of humanity, regardless of gender, has suffered greatly from the loss of feminine awareness. Simply recognizing this loss, moreover, may help us to understand some contemporary dilemmas and sources of controversy and confusion.

In Western society today people feel great insecurity regarding the roles of men and women. Sensing that they are walking on shifting ground, people are uncertain how to think, act, or feel in the presence of the opposite sex. In this shifting environment the safe old rules of behavior are crumbling so swiftly that everyone feels vulnerable, protective, defensive, and cautious.

Though it may not seem so, these painful times are both good and inevitable. As if groaning in the pains of labor, society is experiencing the convulsive contractions preceding the birth of a new millennium.

Who among us even knows how the true, healthy feminine will think, act, or feel? Who among us even knows how the true, healthy masculine will think, act, or feel? All we have are glimpses of this new world of beauty and consciousness.

These privileged glimpses are available largely because of the tenacious inner quest of countless valiant women and men who have searched for their soul, their identity, their destiny. Because of these valiant seekers, we know that the Western world stands on the brink of reclaiming, understanding, and valuing the lost feminine as essential to uniting with the spirit and then giving birth to and nurturing divine values in the world. Similarly, we know that we stand on the brink of redefining and understanding anew the exaggerated masculine, and that this process is essential to moving the culture forward. We are living in exciting times, indeed.

We can be certain that the monumental shift in consciousness that will be required to integrate the feminine soul into a masculine culture—while also redefining, understanding, and valuing the new masculine—will shake society to its very foundations. Life is challenging us all to journey into the shifting, changing land of soul to search for meaning and destiny. Although this journey may at times be frightening and disorienting, we're quickly finding that neither is it safe to attempt standing on our old familiar ground or depending on our old familiar ways of relating.

This great movement in our society will not stand still just because any one person or group of people do not want it to happen. Thus, the issue becomes our response. Will we be creative or fearful? Will we risk the challenge of opportunity, or will we react rigidly? Do we respond with searching questions or inflexible answers? Will we use this opportunity for soul making?

The Formation of Personality

As we examine the many ways our minds guide us and shape our lives—and especially as we do so in the context of understanding the Enneagram and what it has to say to us about freeing our lives and about soul making—we would do well to look at the basic structure of the human mind. Knowing the components of soul and how they interact will lead us one level deeper into soul making.

The human mind has three ways of perceiving the world: thinking, feeling, and doing. It is a formula both ancient and simple, yet it is quite an accurate way of looking at the human person. For example, when we are examining our options in a situation, we will ask ourselves, What do I think about it? How do I feel about it? and What will I do about it?

This interpretation of the human mind is corroborated by the most recent and sophisticated scientific research into the brain. According to these studies, human beings are three-brained beings. The oldest central core of our brains is the reptilian brain, often called the physical brain. The next layer is the mammalian brain, known as the emotional and relational brain. Finally, crowning all is the neocortex, the human brain, or the thinking brain.

These three layers of the human brain develop from the inside out in the earliest years of life. Birth awakens the physical brain, and the emotions are roused a few months later along with awareness of relationships. Finally, physical development allows the baby greater freedom, leading him or her into more complicated situations that require the use of the thinking processes of the intellectual brain.

Research indicates two facts that are central to our study. First, the seat of the ego—our awareness of ourselves as persons—is in the emotional and relational brain. In other words, our primary understanding of ourselves comes from our relationships and emotional experiences. Second, these three brains are meant to be integrated in their functioning, and when they are people operate in a way that promotes well-being for themselves and for the human race.

Perspectives on intelligence. If we begin to think of these three aspects of the person as types of *intelligence,* more becomes clear. Not only is our understanding of human intelligence expanded, but we also come to value aspects of ourselves that need attention in the work of soul making.

Typically, everyone at first glance identifies intelligence with thinking but not necessarily with feeling or doing. Yet when we consider more carefully, we can see that all three of these functions are equally important ways of perceiving, that each gives us both information and capacities that the others cannot give.

For example, thinking establishes laws and rules by which we govern life; without these norms anarchy would reign, and we would have no standards to guide our lives. Feeling, however, examines these laws and rules by applying them to human situations and deciding which are most important in particular situations; without this approach there would be no "give" in human relationships, no sense of valuing the people for whom the laws are made.

With the intelligence of doing, we mobilize our energy to act upon the thoughts and evaluations that proceed from the other two intelligences. Without the will to act, nothing would ever come of all our mental processing; no one would ever benefit from our thoughts or feelings, and the laws and rules we established would never have any real effect upon our lives.

Each of these three intelligences is needed for a person to live a healthy, balanced life. By identifying intelligence with thinking alone, we do ourselves a great disservice. By excluding the kind of intelligence that feeling and doing yield, we prevent ourselves from understanding and using our true potential.

Therefore, let's look into this modern and yet ancient view of human intelligence. In the language of the Enneagram, these three kinds of intelligence—the Intellectual Center (thinking), the Relational Center (feeling), and the

Creative Center (doing)—are the human mind's apparatus for perception and processing of impressions.[3] In them and in comprehending how they function in the human person lies the basis for understanding soul making. Understanding the three centers of intelligence is foundational to perceiving how our primary barrier to soul making, the hidden Original Wound, becomes the source of our Enneagram compulsion.

Balanced Living

Basic to understanding the nine patterns of the Enneagram is the recognition that all people are created with all three centers of intelligence equal and in balance, ready to be used for their appropriate purposes.

The Intellectual Center contains a wellspring, initiating new ideas and original thinking. It also possesses a pure, innocent receptivity that makes it the irresistible

---

[3]In our book *What's My Type?* we used different names for these three centers of intelligence: Theoretical Center for the intelligence of thought and analysis, Affective Center for the intelligence that perceives through feeling, and Effective Center for the intelligence of doing. It was both our evolving understanding of this wisdom and our research that led to the change in terminology here. For example, in his five-volume study of The Work, *Psychological Commentaries on the Teachings of Gurdjieff and Ouspensky* (Boston: Shambhala, 1980), Maurice Nicoll uses the name Intellectual Center. The names Relational Center and Creative Center are our own.

and receptive home of Divine Light. It speaks truth to the individual and society through conscience—the voice of the spirit. This is the center of vision, awareness, and understanding of the true meaning of reality. Its mastery is consciousness.

The Relational Center is the temple of unity and healing. Its vulnerability makes it the irresistible and receptive home of Divine Love. It speaks love to the individual and society by synthesizing and translating the quiet whisperings of intuition—the voice of the soul. Through its power to incarnate, the gifts of the Intellectual Center become visible through words, feeling, symbols, image, and story. Its mastery is process.

The Creative Center contains the expressive vitality of birth, life, death, and rebirth. Its nurturing wisdom makes it the irresistible and receptive home of Divine Life. Through imagination and innovation, it steadily moves toward completing the universal plan for humanity—proclaiming the eternal decree of the Creator. Through freedom, flexibility, and development, it guides the individual and humanity along the narrow way between extremes. Its mastery is creativity.

Unfortunately however, people do not use the three centers properly. Because we are born into an egocentric world, we respond egocentrically to it. This kind of reaction causes us to prefer one center over the other two, thus allowing its way of perceiving and processing impressions to dominate our personality and throw our personality off balance. This preference of one center over the other two is a direct result of our Original Wound.

Preferring one center. The Enneagram clearly indicates which patterns prefer which center; this material is presented pictorially in the diagram "The Centers." Twos, Threes, and Fours prefer the Relational Center, thus becoming overconcerned with the personal dimension of

The Centers

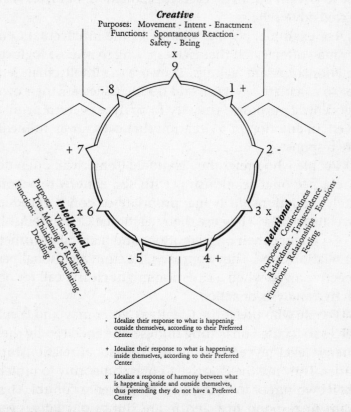

Creative
Purposes: Movement - Intent - Enactment
Functions: Spontaneous Reaction -
Safety - Being

- Idealize their response to what is happening outside themselves, according to their Preferred Center

+ Idealize their response to what is happening inside themselves, according to their Preferred Center

x Idealize a response of harmony between what is happening inside and outside themselves, thus pretending they do not have a Preferred Center

The idea that those to the extreme right and left of each center have something in common with each other comes from lectures by O'Leary and Beesing (Jan. 1986, Denver, CO); the specific descriptions of that commonness are original to Dobson and Hurley, as are the descriptions of the Centers. Copyright © 1992. Enneagram Resources, Inc.

life. Fives, Sixes, and Sevens prefer the Intellectual Center, thus becoming overattentive to developing a rational and information-oriented approach to living. Eights, Nines, and Ones prefer the Creative Center, thus becoming overinterested in the quality of their response to the situations that life presents to them. As we allow one center to govern our lives, each component of our lives is affected adversely.

For example, people who prefer the Intellectual Center may often catch themselves trying to impose logic on relationships and feelings. They use the Intellectual Center to calculate, analyze, and decide issues for their own egocentric purposes. They try to analyze everything first, even an emotion or a situation that calls for an immediate response.

People who prefer the Relational Center will often desire a personal relationship with someone with whom such a relationship is inappropriate or counterproductive, like a boss. They use their Relational Center selfishly to experience their own emotions and manipulate others in relationships. They approach life from a personal perspective, even when a situation might clearly call for objective analysis or action.

People who prefer the Creative Center may find themselves so focused on getting things done and keeping their energy level revved up that their personal relationships suffer. They use the Creative Center stubbornly to protect their own turf or to fight others for power or control. They want to respond first and figure things out later, even though some forethought or awareness of the personal dimension might improve the quality of their response.

Overusing one center.   How do the centers of intelligence slip into the imbalanced state that causes division within and without? As children enter an imperfect world, an egocentric world, they learn to respond to their surroundings. No matter how loving and caring parents might be, they are not perfect; thus the Original Wound is created. Children, who are flexible and able to adapt to their environment, quickly learn the best way to get their needs met. It is in this process that their centers of intelligence gradually slip out of balance.

Initially they adapt to their adult care givers and their immediate environment. Then, as their world expands, they learn how to adapt to more and more people and situations. Eventually children become both comfortable and confident with the familiar pattern that works best for them. The original balance among the centers has been lost; the patterned behavior becomes automatic. They come to perceive, integrate, and understand life— themselves, others, and situations—primarily through the lens of one center of intelligence.

Finding what works for them provides them with many survival skills to use in an often hostile world. It also leads to overuse and distortion of the natural gifts and resources of the center they prefer. They will try to accomplish what that center's resources can't do as well as what it can. This stretching of the center, furthermore, is done only to bypass the challenge of developing the true purposes of another center.

Everyone begins life in balance, gradually slips out of balance in an attempt to adapt to the surroundings, and finally justifies the imbalanced result in themselves, primarily because they don't know they could be any different. In this way we all become addicted to an egocentric, self-serving style of living that we've come to believe is not only normal but also good.

Having entered this cycle of egocentricity, we create disharmony within ourselves and in the world. Until we begin to recognize how this imbalance has created layers and layers of illusion that distort our perception of reality, the cycle will continue, because we see nothing wrong with our perceptions.

People Who Prefer the Relational Center

Twos, Threes, and Fours prefer the Relational Center and therefore, initially and primarily, interpret life through personal feelings and emotions.

The higher purpose of this center is connectedness, relatedness, and transcendence. However, people who prefer this center overuse it so that these aspects of it remain hidden, and the more prosaic functions of the center— feeling, emotion, and relationships—take over.

People who prefer this center tend to personalize issues and relationships, thus taking things personally. Their quick perception on the psychological plane allows them to analyze the human dimension of a person or situation almost instantaneously. Possessing highly developed emotional antennae, they "read" people and situations nonverbally—through tone of voice, mannerisms, or unspoken thoughts, for example. In a situation such as working on a project, if a co-worker's attitude becomes too objective, distant, or focused on completion, people with a preferred Relational Center very often feel threatened and label the other person remote or distant. They will then identify the lack of interaction as proceeding from a personality conflict or poor personal chemistry.

They feel good about themselves when they respond well to people and bad when they don't. Aware of the needs and feelings of others, they attempt to get a favorable response from them. When others respond positively to them, they feel free, responsive, confident, and open; but when they sense rejection or any other negative response they tend to withdraw—sometimes with hurt feelings, sometimes in confusion.

Their deepest concern is their image as it is reflected back to them through others. Overvaluing the Relational Center causes them both to need people around them and to know unconsciously how to manipulate them. Perceiving life primarily as an interpersonal venture creates a constant evaluation of their ability to relate; a deep-seated sense of being unlovable gnaws at them and undermines their sense of self-worth.

People Who Prefer the Intellectual Center

Fives, Sixes, and Sevens prefer the Intellectual Center and therefore, initially and primarily, interpret life through information and knowledge.

The higher purpose of this center is vision, awareness, and grasping the true meaning of reality. However, people who prefer this center overuse it and misuse it by looking at everything, from a complicated math problem to personal relationships, from the same dispassionate point of view—objective interest and impersonal curiosity.

Their interest in asking questions and discussing issues produces a wealth of information with which they then respond to people and situations. When they receive emotionally laden answers to their questions, or when people jump to conclusions, they tend to filter out feelings and gut reactions. They then analyze the information according to a predetermined framework of categories.

They feel good about themselves when they know and analyze information correctly and bad when they don't. If their job, projects, and relationships go well, they interpret these results as an affirmation of their correct analysis of information and thus remain confident, objective, curious, and observant. If complications develop and disrupt their lives, they retreat into their heads, reanalyzing and reorganizing the same information. If they conclude that they were right and others wrong, they become stubbornly determined to prove it.

Overvaluing the Intellectual Center causes them to need to understand where and how they fit into life and its situations. Their logical, impersonal style creates an unconscious sense of superiority. They perceive feelings as unruly and disruptive, as clouding understanding and leading to rash decisions and actions; an air of slight disdain serves as their defense against emotion. Viewing life primarily as an impersonal venture creates an insatiable need for more information; never knowing quite enough makes them feel incapable and erodes their sense of self-confidence.

People Who Prefer the Creative Center

Eights, Nines, and Ones prefer the Creative Center and therefore, initially and primarily, interpret life through a need to act quickly to deal with any situation.

The higher purpose of this center is movement, intent, and enactment. However, people who prefer this center overuse it and misuse it, thus cloaking its true purposes and using their impulse for immediate action as their primary approach to life, people, and situations.

These people know how to react through their "gut feelings." With high expectations regarding self, others, and life in general, their assumption is that everyone should contribute to life by doing something. They develop uncanny skills at perceiving and interpreting physical reality and thus knowing what's going on; often they have a keen sense of shifts that are about to happen in the marketplace.

They feel worthwhile when they have the ability to make a difference in life through their words, actions, and influence and worthless when they don't. If others are up-front, direct, honest, and fair with them, they feel safe, self-assured, and confident. When others' words and actions don't quite match, they begin to feel unsafe and insecure and can become openly hostile.

Overvaluing the Creative Center causes a vague antipathy to life as they know it, an unconscious sense that nothing is the way it should be. Thus, they constantly measure their performance against others' and against the situation. Interminable questioning of their own importance eventually undermines their self-esteem and focuses attention on their inability to change all the aspects of life that they believe need changing.

Different Uses of Preferred Centers

If we compare the descriptions of the nine patterns of the Enneagram in chapter 1 with the depictions of people who prefer each of the centers above, we will notice an interesting and helpful feature. This aspect is presented in the diagram "The Centers" by symbols: a minus sign, a plus sign, or an *x* accompany each number or pattern. We call these variations on the use of Preferred Centers "idealizations" because they describe how each pattern idealizes or makes more important a particular focus for using its Preferred Center. Each of the nine patterns *idealizes* its own distorted perceptions, viewing them as the only valid way of appreciating the world.

The outward idealization. A minus sign marks the Two, the Five, and the Eight. These patterns idealize their response to what is happening *outside* themselves, according to their Preferred Center. By making the outer world the focus of their Preferred Center, they see reality in that world and thereby justify devoting their time and energy to it. Thus, they overemphasize the external experience of their Preferred Center.

Helpers (Twos), who prefer the Relational Center, approach the world in terms of personal feelings and needs. However, their outward idealization causes them to be sensitive to everyone else's feelings and needs while remaining unaware of their own. This external focus creates an inner emptiness that is temporarily filled only when caring for others.

Observers (Fives), who prefer the Intellectual Center, view the world from an abstract or information-oriented perspective. Their outward idealization piques their interest in any knowledge that the world can give them. Even though they are interior people, they ignore the realm of personal feeling and dwell in the world of thought, focusing on outside information that will help them understand how the world operates and where they fit into it.

Confronters (Eights), who prefer the Creative Center, deal with the world through energy and spontaneity. Their outward idealization propels them to use their tremendous vitality for accepting and surmounting every challenge the world offers. Simultaneously, however, they find introspection difficult, for the interior life feels lonely, barren, and fearful.

The inward idealization. A plus sign marks the Four, the Seven, and the One. These patterns idealize their response to what is happening *inside* themselves, according to their Preferred Center. By making the inner world the focus of their Preferred Center, they see reality as happening within and thereby justify turning their time and energy in this direction. Thus, they overemphasize the internal experience of their Preferred Center.

Individualists (Fours), who prefer the Relational Center, approach the world in terms of personal feelings and needs. However, their inward idealization causes them to be sensitive to their own feelings and needs first and only then to other people's. Their great desire is to understand themselves and to be understood by one other person.

Dreamers (Sevens), who prefer the Intellectual Center, view the world in terms of thoughts and ideas. Their inward idealization causes their minds to whir in high gear with schemes and plans to improve their own lives but also to find solutions for other people's problems. Dreamers want to live in a happy, pain-free world.

Achievers (Ones), who prefer the Creative Center, deal with the world through energy and intensity of response. Their inward idealization focuses their reactions like a laser beam in their own lives, as they attempt with determination and willpower to create perfection in a chaotic world. They carry a burden that does not belong to them and is too heavy for anyone to bear.

The balancing idealization. The final group—and in some ways the most troublesome to understand—are those that are marked with an *x:* the Three, the Six, and the Nine. Called the Balance Points, these patterns idealize their ability to *harmonize* or *balance* what is happening inside and outside themselves, according to their Preferred Center.

They accomplish this goal by doing something quite different and surprising: *they repress the use of their Preferred Center.* Though they have a Preferred Center, they use only its outward shell in an attempt to be all things to all people. If they made a commitment to use the center completely, they could not remain in harmony with others and with the world.

The result is that they have equal access to all three centers (represented in the Enneagram by the equilateral triangle that connects them) but, like everyone else, live in compulsion because they use none of the centers for its true purpose. Reality for these three patterns lies in their ability to be in balance with everything at all times. They overemphasize the importance of equilibrium with every person and every situation, according to their Preferred Center.

Succeeders (Threes) both prefer and repress the Relational Center; consequently they live in a world in which their own feelings are rarely honored and their own needs rarely met. While glowing with the relational warmth of this center, they may never get beyond perceiving and meeting the surface feelings and needs of others. By repressing the personal realm, they are able to focus on work, proficiency, and productivity, thereby enhancing their appearance of confidence, competence, and capability. Having repressed their sensitivity to self and others, they focus on accomplishing goals that lead to success, not on developing substantial relationships.

Guardians (Sixes) both prefer and repress the Intellectual Center; consequently they live in a world in which their objectivity feels constantly compromised by the social situation. Exuding the curiosity of this center, their constant questioning of themselves and others creates an anxiety that there are no sure answers in life. Thus, they connect with a group to create a social niche where they can feel comfortable, conforming to it and taking its standards for their own. Mistrustful of any single person's ideas or opinions, they increase their ties with the group as a whole by seeking multiple confirmations of their own value or of ideas and plans. Activity and responsibility in the community give them the security and sense of belonging they seek.

Preservationists (Nines) both prefer and repress the Creative Center; consequently silence and stamina are their only defense against the onslaught of the world. Emanating the strength of this center, they use their power to stop life from happening in the personal realm, thus establishing a safe, unchanging environment. Having repressed their own energy, they use stubbornness to keep from dealing with issues or problems, primarily in their private lives. They expect others to handle problems while ignoring anything they find disagreeable. They use their energy socially and professionally to create a good reputation, in play and outdoor activities, for games and fun, and in the personal realm to stave off unpleasantness.

The enigma of the Three, Six, and Nine. Because they repress their Preferred Center, this last group—the Balance Points—are often seen as a confusing enigma by themselves and others. Preferring and repressing the same center, they would seem to possess shallow personalities, but meeting them disproves that thought immediately. Who are they? Through what lens do they perceive and interpret life? These are some of the questions that will be addressed in the next chapter, and they will guide us to a deeper understanding of all nine types described by the Enneagram. Then we will see how in the Enneagram Riddle (see the Introduction) *nine become twelve.*

Waters of the Mind

From time immemorial, water has been recognized as symbolic of both the mind and the feminine element in creation. The title of the song *Ol' Man River* notwithstanding, water as a feminine symbol remains a constant throughout the history of human thought. In the ancient cultures of the Orient, water was called *The Great Mother of All Life* because all living cells began in her depths.

Expressed in the language of modern psychology, water is the symbol of the unconscious mind and of the feminine principle in the personality. It is a symbol of the soul.

Ancient cultures saw water as the connecting principle between heaven and earth. Water is symbolically the mediator between the world of spirit and the material world; applied to the person, the meaning is clear: soul connects spirit with body. As the intuitive wisdom of the Divine

Mother, water becomes a metaphor for the creative wisdom of the mind because it doesn't struggle against barriers. Instead, it flows around obstacles, much as a stream flows around rocks and boulders rather than pushing through them, on the one hand, or being confined by them, on the other. Yet, if a dam is constructed, the water will stop, waiting for an opening to be offered.

The struggle of soul making, then, is to question, search, and wait on the shores of the dark, chaotic waters of the unconscious until wisdom emerges. Once it is grasped, there follows the hard work of forming a language that can communicate this wisdom to the conscious mind in a way that can be understood.

A person's efforts, then, must first be directed toward learning how to listen to the soul's voice of intuition. Next comes the work of interpreting what has been seen and heard in the inner world in such a way that it can be spoken in the physical world. At this point *fire enters the water* so that the vision can be clearly seen and understood.

Being alone and still, then, is the beginning of the wisdom that will reveal the imbalance of our lives and what to do about it. These life-giving, regenerating waters will speak to us of our interior lives, relationships, life goals, and dreams. They will unveil the lassitude that arises from lack of guidance in our lives and reveal the ways that cynicism has masqueraded as practicality, that we have justified dashing our own dream of living a life of excellence on the rocks of making a living and feeling good in the moment.

When it becomes painful to recognize the specific ways we give in to the illusions created by preferring one kind of intelligence and we need to be comforted and refreshed, it is in the aloneness within that we can discover the idealism, the discipline, and the guidance that will convey the life of the soul into our daily existence. Through this everyday work of soul making, wisdom, love, and creativity gently seep into our lives and transformation begins.

For Personal and Group Work

1. Identify your Preferred Center of intelligence and reflect on how it limits and focuses your perspective on life. Preferring one kind of intelligence leads to ignoring the information from the other two intelligences to various degrees. Notice that this is especially true when a person is backed against the wall and feels defensive. At these times it is normal for people to rely on what they perceive to be their strengths; often these are qualities that arise from overusing the Preferred Center.

Think of a recent disagreement you were involved in, and take a new look at the things you thought, felt, and did, seeing how they were influenced by your Preferred Center. How would you have thought, felt, or acted differently if all three centers were in balance within you?

2. Look at three valued personal relationships in your life. Are they with people who seem to prefer the same center as you, or are they with people who prefer a different kind of intelligence? What are the strengths and weaknesses you see in each relationship that arise from sharing a Preferred Center, or from preferring different centers?

3. All of us in our society—women as well as men—are encouraged to live out of a shallow definition of the masculine that focuses on accomplishment, achievement, keeping busy, and consumption of material goods; doing so fuels our Enneagram compulsion and keeps us operating on a mechanical level. However, the true feminine is emerging in our lives as well through respect for experience, emotion, feeling, personal knowledge, interconnecting, equality, partnership, understanding of relationship and intimacy, personal and collective validation of history or myth, images, imagination, humor, the freedom to question and investigate, and consciousness. These feminine ways of understanding connect us to and reveal the Divine Feminine in all creation. Choose three of these qualities and describe the ways they have been emerging in your life.

4. Reflecting on your life, how has water—a river, a pond, a lake, an ocean, or rain in an overflowing rain barrel—played a part in your life? Are your memories positive or negative—for example, happy, sad, peaceful, relaxing, hectic? What positive values could meditating on water help you reclaim? What meaningful values are now present in your life that you could consciously build on and strengthen?

3

Questioning: Reclaiming a Lost Art

When you have eliminated the impossible,
whatever remains, however improbable,
must be the truth.

—SIR ARTHUR CONAN DOYLE

It is fascinating to realize how many times comments like "It's impossible," "It's a mystery," or "We aren't meant to understand it, just accept" are not only used but welcomed, even by very bright individuals, as perfectly rational. Once something is accepted as impossible or as an inexplicable mystery, all questioning and exploration cease.

What would happen, though, if a person were not informed that something was impossible? Would it then become possible?

One day a young graduate student ran into his statistics class at the University of California at Berkeley, breathless and very late. In fact, the class was nearly over. There were two problems written on the board that he assumed were that day's assignment. He copied them down and, working long hours over the weekend, finally completed and turned in his assignment.

Less than two months later, the professor of his statistics class arrived at his door with a manuscript that he wanted the young man to sign. The manuscript centered on the two problems he had hurriedly copied off the board and turned in weeks earlier.

The professor, as it turned out, had simply written those problems on the board as examples of unsolvable math problems. Since the time of Einstein, the experts had all agreed that these problems were impossible to solve. The student, George B. Dantzig, is known today as the father of linear programming. Because a student failed to hear the word *impossible,* his mind—free to explore and question—discovered the possible.

The word *question* comes from the Latin *quaerere* meaning "to seek" or "to quest." It was a question that led us on a search into the wisdom of the Enneagram to solve what appeared to be an impossible dilemma. The quest, which spanned several years, did finally lead to an entirely new perspective on the Enneagram.

In the last chapter we described the Balance Point Numbers—Succeeders (Threes), Guardians (Sixes), and Preservationists (Nines)—noting that the surprising way their personalities were formed, that is, by repressing their Preferred Center, would be the key to deeper understanding for all nine patterns of the Enneagram. One way to understand what it means for these patterns to prefer and repress the same center is to say that they manifest only the outer shell of their Preferred Center but not its core. But what does this mean in terms of daily living for people of these three patterns?

Earlier we suggested that preferring one center is the basis around which personality forms. If the Preferred Center is the basis for personality formation and these patterns repress their Preferred Center, what is the basis for their personality? Who are they? Through what lens, what center of intelligence, do they perceive and interpret life? How do they relate to other people, to themselves, and to the world? Why do they seem so complex and difficult to understand?

Surely we know from human experience that people with these three patterns are definitely not devoid of personality. Furthermore, there is a wide range of variation in the ways people express these types. What can all this mean?

Repressing and Expressing

When we take a look at these three patterns using what we know of the centers as our guide, what we find may at first be a confusing surprise. In general these patterns, even as they repress their own Preferred Center, do express the other two centers rather well.

For example, Succeeders (Threes), who prefer but repress the Relational Center, glow with a personal warmth that often masks a bottom-line attitude toward accomplishing tasks and achieving goals. Though appearing friendly, they don't easily form close or intimate relationships and have difficulty expressing emotion. As they hide behind the shell of the personal Relational Center, their life direction, when they are caught in their compulsion, is rather impersonal.

However, what Succeeders do well is use the Intellectual Center as they think through and plan their goals, and they are active people who accomplish their goals, thus displaying ample experience with the Creative Center. If you reexamine any description of Succeeders, you will find this formula underlying it: the shell of the Relational Center is filled with qualities from the calculating Intellectual Center and the productive Creative Center.

Similarly, Guardians (Sixes), who prefer but repress the Intellectual Center, want to be known as responsible members of the community who are "in the know," an attitude that masks their deep-seated insecurity. They don't easily think through issues for themselves and have difficulty validating their own point of view. Hiding behind the shell of the information-oriented Intellectual Center, when they are caught in their compulsion, they are driven to validate information over and over again because they mistrust it.

However, what Guardians do well is use the Creative Center as they schedule their lives with activity and responsibilities that put them at the heart of their prime reference group, and they are relational people who network and are proud of their many connections and ties with people, underscoring their substantial use of the Relational Center. If you reexamine any portrait of Guardians, you will find this formula underlying it: the shell of the fact-oriented Intellectual Center is filled with qualities from the energetic Creative Center and the relationship-oriented Relational Center.

Finally, Preservationists (Nines), who prefer but repress the Creative Center, present to the world both the fun-loving and the stubborn qualities that one would associate with a dynamic person but that for them disguise their desire to keep things as they are. They don't easily deal with the tough issues of life, preferring to sidestep or ignore them. Hiding behind the shell of the energy-oriented Creative Center, when they are caught in their compulsion, they retreat from exerting their strength on the real issues of life into a *che sarà, sarà*—what will be, will be—attitude.

However, what Preservationists do well is use the impersonal Intellectual Center to solve problems in the external world and are often creative thinkers with original ideas. Also, they are affable people who are generally well liked and socially appreciated, indicating their familiarity with the functions of the Relational Center. If you reexamine any description of Preservationists you will find this formula underlying it: the shell of the action-oriented Creative Center is filled with qualities from the objective Intellectual Center and the image-oriented Relational Center.

One Center Is Preferred; Another Dominates

Recognizing that the Balance Point numbers—Threes, Sixes, and Nines—seem to allow the other two centers to dominate the expression of their pattern leads us to an insight into the Enneagram that, until now, no one has articulated. Besides the importance of the Preferred Center in formation of personality, each pattern has a *Dominant Center* that influences it as well. For six of the nine patterns—Twos, Fours, Fives, Sevens, Eights, and Ones—the Preferred Center is also the Dominant Center and therefore is the commanding factor in the creation of personality and the setting of lifestyle.

But for Threes, Sixes, and Nines, a different scenario emerges, and with it comes a more refined understanding of the different ways we experience these three types in daily life. For them, because the Preferred Center is repressed, one of the other two centers dominates.

Thus, each of these patterns contains two distinct subgroups, each with a different Dominant Center around which the personality is formed. Therefore, there are two kinds of Threes: Intellectual Threes and Creative Threes; two kinds of Sixes: Relational Sixes and Creative Sixes; and two kinds of Nines: Intellectual Nines and Relational Nines. In this way, in the Enneagram Riddle (see the Introduction) *nine become twelve.*

Two Kinds of Threes

Intellectual Threes. Succeeders in whom the Intellectual Center dominates possess the qualities associated with Threes but express them through the lens of the Dominant Intellectual Center. Intellectual Threes are quieter and less flashy than Creative Threes. They probably tend to be more introverted, idealistic, and less confident when it comes to actualizing their ideals in the world.

Often highly intuitive and filled with ideas, possibilities, and new concepts, they focus their leadership on initiating enthusiasm in others, helping them catch a vision of future opportunities so that they will want to work hard to be a part of that future.

Because they are more inwardly focused, they find initiating and maintaining relationships more difficult. They are less approachable and trusting of others than their Creative-centered counterparts. Therefore, their demeanor is more aloof and superior, and they are more intense, serious, and dedicated. They are the kind of people who get an idea and transform it into a vision that will inspire them for years.

When they want to motivate others, they will be inclined to read books to discover the best method. Because their focus is more interior, they apply their realistic and practical nature to the world of ideas as well as to the spiritual world—thus, lack of authenticity and charlatanism are frequently transparent to them, as are other people's motives in general.

Creative Threes.   Succeeders in whom the Creative Center dominates possess all the qualities associated with Threes but express them through the lens of their Dominant Creative Center. Usually more extroverted than their Intellectual-centered counterparts, they know how to get the ball rolling in their own lives and the lives of those around them. An innate knowledge of how to get things done in the outer world allows them to move with apparent ease in business and social circles. Often direct in communication and lighthearted in their public profile, they are approachable, down to earth, easy to be with—less intense and serious than Intellectual Threes.

Because they are outwardly focused, they initiate and maintain relationships easily. Well grounded in reality and common sense, secretly they often develop a skeptical, even cynical attitude toward life. Their ability to manipulate material reality and even people causes others to look to them for leadership, which Creative Threes find both natural and challenging.

In learning how to motivate others, they will spend time with people and through questioning and dialogue discover the most effective method. Their focus being more outward, they apply their realistic and practical nature to the material world—making things happen and keeping life exciting will be their forte.

Two Kinds of Sixes

Relational Sixes.   Guardians in whom the Relational Center dominates possess all the qualities associated with Sixes by express them through the lens of their Dominant Relational Center. They are quieter people, more sensitive to feelings and relationships than their Creative-centered counterparts, and thus often more introverted. Their world will also be smaller—fewer relationships with stronger ties, and they will be only mildly interested in anything that does not directly affect them or those close to them.

If they are parents, they will sacrifice their desires, dreams, and happiness to ensure that their children will have a better life than they had, but their fear may prevent them from pursuing their own happiness. Consequently, they are apt to live vicariously through the achievements of those whom they love. These attitudes will motivate them to be at the heart of the family or the prime reference group in their lives.

In the comfort of their own surroundings, their strength is obvious and graciousness reigns whenever they welcome people into their home. However, they feel less confident in larger social gatherings than their Creative-centered counterparts. In decision making they depend on people who are important to them to affirm their ideas and back them up. The object of their insecurity is often primarily financial, thus making them more economically conservative and more worrisome about the future than the people around them, while they will often take their own physical health for granted.

All Sixes are opinionated, but Relational Sixes use their convictions primarily to guide their actions or to instill moral values in people close to them. In public they tend to keep silent about their opinions but in private they express their outrage and frustration about others' opposing viewpoints to a trusted friend.

Creative Sixes. Guardians in whom the Creative Center dominates possess all the qualities associated with Sixes but express them through the lens of their Dominant Creative Center. These are blunt, direct, active, outgoing people, often more extroverted than their Relational-centered counterparts.

They know how to connect with the "right" people, who will enhance their own respectability. By maintaining full social schedules, they can become known as the life of the party. They are impressed by elegant and distinctive gatherings and themselves tend to be more lavish, extravagant spenders.

Somewhat insensitive to subtleties in relationship, they can be quite aggressive, especially when they are on their own turf. They often communicate their strong values with a sharp humor that can make them devastating opponents as well as lifelong friends. Though their family ties are important to them, they may be less self-sacrificial and more self-indulgent in the way they live, since they are attuned to their physical well-being.

Openly opinionated, they place many demands on others and are not very tolerant of people whose values are different from their own. By speaking their minds freely, they stick their foot in their mouth more often than their Relational-centered counterparts. These are practical, realistic people whose business sense and common sense make them valued members of the community.

Two Kinds of Nines

Intellectual Nines.   Preservationists in whom the Intellectual Center dominates possess all the qualities associated with Nines but express them through the lens of their Dominant Intellectual Center. Often more distant and objective, less relational and responsive than their Relational-centered counterparts, they tend to be introverted. Being somewhat absentminded, they can be forgetful of personal obligations and responsibilities. They are less sensitive to feelings—other people's or their own—and often are unconcerned about their personal appearance, even taking pride in their casual, rumpled, or eccentric style.

Living in a somewhat impersonal world, they are often unaware of how their words and actions affect others. They experience great discomfort when pressed to disclose personal needs or feelings. Quiet people, they spend a great deal of time alone, simply thinking or involved with a favorite craft, hobby, or activity.

Objective in approach, their analytical powers are liberated when set upon practical, impersonal problems. They are often attracted to technical occupations or avocations in which these abilities are respected and used. If they like to read, they prefer reading professional journals, general information magazines, or material related to their favorite hobby or sport.

Relational Nines.   Preservationists in whom the Relational Center dominates possess all the qualities associated with Nines but express them through the lens of their Dominant Relational Center. Being more extroverted than their Intellectual-centered counterparts, these are friendly, social people who know how to connect personally with others. They take other people's feelings and circumstances into account when making a decision. Attentive to their personal appearance and image, they often have a sensual air about them.

Being aware of emotions and relationships, they know that their words and actions affect others. Thus, they put effort into learning communication skills and, even though it makes them somewhat uncomfortable, are able to disclose personal information. People enjoy being with them socially, and they are well respected in their work community.

Because they are interested in people, easy to get along with, and generally unflappable, they enjoy occupations and avocations that others might consider emotionally stressful. They apply their native stamina easily to human needs and problems. If they like to read, they often prefer books on psychology and personal growth, biographies, and reading about people and their relationships.

Dominant Center for Wing Numbers

In distinction to the Balance Point Numbers, Twos, Fours, Fives, Sevens, Eights, and Ones are called Wing Numbers because they are on the outer edges, or wings, of each center. For these types, the Preferred Center and Dominant Center are the same.

The Relational Center dominates the personalities of Helpers (Twos) and Individualists (Fours), who are pre-eminently concerned with relationships, emotions, and the human situation. Concern for personal needs—their own and others'—is uppermost in their minds. By being too intensely involved in relationships, they develop dependency in others or themselves that inevitably causes arguments, hurt feelings, and broken relationships.

The Intellectual Center dominates the personalities of Observers (Fives) and Dreamers (Sevens), who have overactive minds—gathering information, thinking, analyzing, and calculating. Remaining impersonal and objective, even in the midst of a relationship, is a deep need in them. They get so caught up in the world of ideas, their own and other people's, they can spin their wheels and never quite accomplish anything of substance.

The Creative Center dominates the personalities of Confronters (Eights) and Achievers (Ones), who are intensely invested in doing. Eights are easily bored and feel they need to light a fire under others to keep life interesting. Ones are preoccupied with doing things right and working hard to improve the world. Both become so overwhelmed with the need for activity they can miss the beauty in the world, in themselves, and in others.

Summary.   For all nine types in the Enneagram, the *Preferred Center* is the source of *unconscious motivation*. It could be likened to the engine of an automobile. It's running all the time, and although you don't see it, it houses the power that keeps the car—the compulsion—constantly in motion.

The *Dominant Center* is the source of *expression* for the unconscious motivation. The expression could be likened to the chassis, the paint, and the upholstery of the car. It's what you see, how you identify it, and what you like or dislike—it's the person's personality as expressed in the outer world.

Although there are just nine engines or types of unconscious motivations in the Enneagram, there are twelve chassis, or expressions. For the Balance Point Numbers—Threes, Sixes, and Nines—the Dominant Center and the

Preferred Center are different from each other. In all the other numbers, the Wing Numbers—Twos, Fours, Fives, Sevens, Eights, and Ones—the Preferred and Dominant Centers are the same.

The Valuable Support Center

The Support Center of intelligence for Wing Numbers is simple to identify. Locate your number on the diagram in chapter 2 called "The Centers." Your Preferred and Dominant Center is the center in which your number resides; your Support Center is the center (not the number or type) next to your number. The Support Center for Balance Point Numbers is identified in a different way. These numbers have already identified their Preferred Center and Dominant Center, which are different from each other. Their Support Center is the remaining one.

Recognition and understanding of the Support Center of intelligence is important for several reasons. First, remembering that *every person is one and only one Enneagram type,* because a type is essentially about motivation, many of the qualities of any or all of the three numbers in each type's Support Center can fill out a person's personality. The variety of these additional qualities helps us to comprehend and explain the great diversity found among people who have the same Enneagram numbers.

Second, the qualities that emerge from the Support Center are most often positive strengths we can draw upon to assist us in overcoming compulsive attitudes in our daily lives.

Third, observing how we use our Support Center can be a great factor in motivating us to work hard at neutralizing our compulsions because this is our healthiest center of intelligence. *This center is healthy because we are not egocentrically invested in its use.*

Almost without exception we've found that when people recall the qualities and virtues that others have most admired and complimented them on ever since childhood, these positive qualities are the natural resources of their Support or Secondary Center. Recognizing the positive results of gifts and talents used freely—devoid of egocentric motives—gives reason and impetus to become free of egocentricity in other areas of our lives.

Summary.   In the Wing Numbers, the Preferred Center of unconscious motivation and the Dominant Center, which gives expression to the personality in the outer world, are the same. The Support Center of intelligence is the center next to the number. The center in which a Wing Number resides is its Preferred/Dominant Center.

For the Balance Point Numbers, the source of unconscious motivation, which lies in the Preferred Center, is consistent. However, the compulsive expression of the unconscious motivation is mediated through one of the other two centers. The center that gives compulsive expression to the personality in the outer world is called the Dominant Center. The remaining center—neither the

Preferred nor the Dominant Center—is the Secondary or Support Center.

The Gift of Questions

Every quest—personal, spiritual, scientific, moral, or religious—begins because someone has the courage to question commonly accepted beliefs. Questioning itself is an art that all but a few rare individuals lost in childhood. Those adults who have a gift for asking questions—and we all have known someone who questions well—have reclaimed a treasure. Through tenacious practice, they have learned—just as we can learn—how to question so as to pierce through to the hidden world of soul.

As children, we asked questions as a way of trying to understand what life was about. Instead, because we were given answers, most of us came to believe that answers were more important than questions. It was the rare child who was blessed by the parental wisdom and guidance described in the following story from Donald Sheff in a letter to *The New York Times:*

> Isidor I. Rabi, the Nobel laureate in physics, was once asked: "Why did you become a scientist rather than a doctor or lawyer or businessman, like the other immigrant kids in your neighborhood?" Dr. Rabi's answer was: "My mother made me a scientist without ever intending it. Every other Jewish mother in Brooklyn would ask her child after school: 'So! Did you learn anything today?' But not my mother. She always asked

me a different question. 'Izzy,' she would say, 'did you ask a good question today?' That difference—'asking good questions'—made me become a scientist!"[1]

Being natural soul makers, children ask questions as a way of understanding, for understanding opens the windows of the soul. Most often, because adults respond with obvious answers, children ask again, and again, and again—until either they finally understand or are sent away by a frustrated adult. In the end, however, nearly all children learn to stop asking questions and become conditioned to expect, accept, and repeat answers. Yet that insistent, curious, questioning, little soul-making child continues to live within every answer-oriented adult, who therefore may choose to once again become a natural soul maker.

For Personal and Group Work

1. Questions open the door to potentials and possibilities. Can you think of a time in your life when, by asking a new or different question, you were able to get around an obstacle and break forth into a new freedom for yourself? What did you learn about yourself, your inner resources, and the world you live in through that process? How did that lesson change your approach to other life situations?

---

[1]As reprinted in *The ABC's of the Human Mind*, ed. Alma E. Guinness, (Pleasantville, NY: The Reader's Digest Association, 1990), p. 249.

2. Some people feel threatened or resentful when questioned in any way. Others feel embarrassed at the thought of asking a question. Still others feel fear or guilt at the idea of questioning those they evaluate as superior to them.

If you fall into any of these categories in any area of your life, have you ever wondered why? Do you feel that your attitude toward questioning has been a detriment? Do you remember asking questions as a child? If so, do you know when you stopped or why?

Sometimes, people who will not verbalize questions still question things internally. Are you one of these people? The art of questioning is natural to children; what steps could you take to reclaim that art, either internally or externally, in your life?

3. Identify your Dominant Center of intelligence. Each of the three centers is a composite of many gifts and strengths, which only become liabilities when they are overused and therefore distorted. What are the gifts and strengths that your Dominant Center lends to your personality? What are the particular and unique ways you use these qualities? In what situations, under what pressures, do you overuse and therefore distort these qualities into weaknesses for yourself? How do both the strengths and weaknesses that flow from your Dominant Center shape the way you express your personality?

4. Identify the talents and gifts you have received most praise for during your life. Now identify your Support Center. Very often people experience this center as the origin of the talents and gifts they have been praised for. How is this notion true for you?

4

Inside Out and Upside Down

Work of the eyes is done, now
Go and do heart-work.
—RANIER MARIA RILKE

American artist Bev Doolittle has developed a unique painting style that she calls her "camouflage technique." In this process she feels free to break all the standard rules of artistic composition. For example, in *Woodland Encounter* she placed a brightly colored fox directly in the center background. Even a neophyte in the world of art knows that you never center anything in a painting and that the attention should always be drawn to the foreground first, then to the middle ground, and finally to the background.

By turning the rules inside out, Doolittle cleverly distracts the viewer from seeing the more important and interesting happenings—Indians on pinto ponies creeping stealthily through the silent woods—camouflaged in the foreground of her surrounding snowscape. The result is that the viewer is given the delightful experience of discovering the hidden in the midst of the obvious.

Through many years of silently observing nature and learning how to "listen with my eyes," Doolittle discovered one of life's greatest secrets: the obvious things in life are distractions that lull us into believing reality lies only in the physical world and, therefore, can only be experienced through the five senses. If Doolittle had failed to question the possibility of another dimension of reality hidden beneath the surface, both she and the world would have been denied the life-enhancing gift of her paintings.

The temptation when hearing a story of triumph like Doolittle's is to regard her as one of those special people who have been blessed with a great destiny. Although she *is* special and blessed, it would be a mistake to regard her as more special or more blessed than anyone else. *All* have been given a great destiny, and each individual's destiny is unique. Until we are courageous enough to begin questioning and searching for truth that is camouflaged in the many experiences and trappings of our lives, our destiny will remain hidden from us. Even as we wistfully listen to other people's stories, we will continue to be unconscious of the fact that our own story remains unwritten.

Our personal story of blessing, greatness, and destiny will never have a beginning until we become comfortable with open-ended questions. The great difficulty with them is that *they have no answers* and *they are constantly changing.* They grow in newness as rapidly as the person who is asking.

Therein lies both the blessing and the curse. For questions like these are sacred and bear no resemblance to questions with answers. From the time we were children we were trained to believe that questions, though important, were only a means to an end. Because the ultimate goal was always to possess the answer, that's where we placed our faith, and upon those answers we built our lives.

Whenever we place our faith and build our lives on rigid answers rather than flexible questions we can be certain that sooner or later we will waste a great deal of our life energy defending those answers. Yet because rigid answers create the illusion of safety, security, and life, we close our eyes and wrap our answers around us as tightly as we would a raincoat on a dark and stormy night.

Thus, just as it is rare to notice the flashing light of a firefly during the day, it is rare for people to recognize the flickering light of Sacred Questions when their lives are filled with blue skies and sunshine. In every life, however, storm clouds and darkness will inevitably descend like a gigantic shroud, blotting out the light-filled world we've taken for granted.

The moment that our life is whipped by the winds of change that turn it inside out and upside down is usually the moment that the true story of our life—of who we were created to be—begins to be written. If we choose to pursue the flickering light of the sacred—and it is always a choice, even if a choice born of desperation—we find that our life has never been what it appeared to be.

As we learn to listen with our eyes, see with our hearts, and speak without words, layer upon layer of illusion dry up and blow away. At last, standing on the Great Bridge of our own soul, we'll discover the world of mystery, beauty, symbol, and story, a world where wounds are gifts, where darkness is dispelled through the light of understanding, and where what is true is recognizable only because it is ever-changing.

Moving Toward the Vision

The purpose of the Enneagram is to establish unity, unity within the person, among people, and within the whole of creation. Everything that ever has or ever will be created begins through union. Human life begins with the union of egg and sperm. A tree grows because a seed unites with the earth. The greatest artist ever born becomes an artist only when the inner visions of sight or sound are united with canvas, clay, musical score, dance, or some other external medium of expression.

Without union, there exists only the potential for creation, which, unless united with another element, will disintegrate. Potential must either unite, integrate, create, and multiply, or it will isolate, disintegrate, and die. Alone, the egg and sperm will die, the seed will rot, and the inner visions of the artist, like dew under the morning sun, will dry up and vanish in silence.

The Enneagram teaches us that people are created with all three centers of intelligence *in balance, but not united.* In the process of growth they first become imbalanced and we become compulsive. As we learn the lessons we need to learn from this stage in life, we accept the need to balance all three centers. If the desire to learn about ourselves is to have any meaning, we must look beyond the unhealthy fascination with death to the creative challenge and beauty of life. In the wisdom of the Enneagram, the potential for creative growth and life is stored in our three centers of intelligence. In these three centers lie the seeds of universal harmony—seeds of faith, hope, and love.

Whether a vision is personal or universal, it can only become real by starting where we are and moving toward it one step at a time. To move toward the vision of unity in our three centers of intelligence we begin where we are—in their compulsive and imbalanced use.

In the last chapter we examined the Preferred Center, the Dominant Center, and the Support Center. Little has been said so far, in this or any other treatment of the Enneagram, about the remaining center, the Repressed Center. What is it? What part does it play in our everyday life? Like the artist Doolittle, can we look beneath the surface, turn the Enneagram inside out and our notions about it upside down, and learn something about our lives?

The Repressed Center

As we allow one center of intelligence to dominate our personalities by overusing it and use a second center to support our Dominant Center, we repress the final center and use it very little. The Repressed Center of intelligence is the center we dislike the most, understand the least, and avoid with great cunning and agility. It is not surprising that we ignore this center of intelligence; because we are not familiar with it, even cautious, infrequent use of the Repressed Center usually leads to feelings of humiliation and failure.

As we examine our lives, we find *the effects of repressing a center will primarily be evident in our personal lives.* In our public lives—especially on the job, whether in the marketplace or in the seclusion of our own home, but also in our social contacts—we learn whatever is necessary to get along or to get ahead. In private, however, we can just relax and be our real selves.

At home, no longer having to wear the public mask or play games, we let down our guard, and the contents of our Repressed Center suddenly leap free from the dark unconscious. Just when we think we have a safe place to unwind, unexpected shadows begin to weave dissension in and out of all our relationships. Because we don't recognize the shadows of our own Repressed Center, we self-righteously wonder why other people are being so unreasonable.

If we are to creatively unite all three centers and become fully human, we must first bring these three centers into balance. Therefore, though it is helpful to identify the ways we overuse our Dominant Center and take corrective measures, *we must direct our efforts to grow in consciousness toward our Repressed Center.* Developing its repressed qualities will necessarily bring the overused centers into alignment.

To look at ourselves objectively—without being critical or condemning—requires a good bit of stamina and determination. Yet, if we are willing to examine our personality, we will begin to see through our illusions and perceive a reality that was previously hidden from us. Every time we look at ourselves with honesty and sincerity, we shed the light of truth and consciousness on the path that leads us more deeply into the land of soul— into the land of the Great Bridge.

You can identify your Dominant, Support, and Repressed Centers in the following chart.

Center Configuration for the Nine Enneagram Patterns

Pattern	Dominant Center	Support Center	Repressed Center
1. Achiever	Creative	Relational	Intellectual
2. Helper	Relational	Creative	Intellectual
3. Succeeder	Intellectual or Creative	Creative or Intellectual	Relational
4. Individualist	Relational	Intellectual	Creative
5. Observer	Intellectual	Relational	Creative
6. Guardian	Creative or Relational	Relational or Creative	Intellectual
7. Dreamer	Intellectual	Creative	Relational
8. Confronter	Creative	Intellectual	Relational
9. Preservationist	Relational or Intellectual	Intellectual or Relational	Creative

Common Repressed Center

This chart suggests we can look at the Enneagram from a new and exciting perspective, namely, by grouping types according to which center they repress. In doing so, in a sense we turn the Enneagram inside out, and we look at each type from the inside out, that is, from the perspective of the qualities that are *missing* instead of only the qualities that are *apparent*. By taking this different perspective, we gain new insight—not only into why each type is the way it is, but even more importantly into the practical steps we each can take to move toward maturity and communion.

Patterns that have the same Repressed Center have important characteristics in common. From this perspective Threes, Sevens, and Eights take an aggressive stance toward life because they have a common Repressed Relational Center. Ones, Twos, and Sixes take a dependent stance toward life because they have a common Repressed Intellectual Center. Fours, Fives, and Nines take a withdrawing stance toward life because they have all repressed the Creative Center.[1]

---

[1]In our book *What's My Type?* we introduced the notion of the Aggressive, Dependent, and Withdrawing Stance in chapter 3. Here we expand on those ideas, using them as a basis for new thinking, namely, seeing that their genesis lies in the Repressed Center. These three categories are not unique to us, although our insight into them is uniquely our own. O'Leary, Beesing, and Nogosek use these categories in *The Enneagram: A Journey of Self-discovery* (Denville, NJ: Dimension Books, 1984), as does Don Richard Riso in *Personality Types: Using the Enneagram for Self-discovery* (Boston: Houghton Mifflin, 1987). Our way of grouping types in these categories corresponds to Riso's, though we have a different way of explaining the reasoning behind the groupings.

The Aggressive Stance.   Threes, Sevens, and Eights are known as the aggressive patterns. Focusing on accomplishing—getting things done and making things happen—their desire is to mold the world to their way of thinking. Their deepest goal is to effect change, so they look for results. What is missing in the Aggressive Stance is the personal approach.

The reason that these patterns become aggressive in these ways is that they all repress the Relational Center. The Relational is the center of feeling, emotion, and relationship; through it, people enter and function in the personal world. If you repress the importance of emotions and relationships, as these patterns do, the Aggressive Stance becomes not only possible but indeed inevitable.

With the importance of personal values ignored, these patterns easily justify manipulating the world to get their own way. If your own needs and feelings are not important and other people's needs and feelings are inconsequential, you have every right to drive yourself and others for the sake of effecting change in the world. If the personal realm is insignificant, you don't need to spend time on relationships. You can keep on thinking or working or playing—whatever you want to do.

Their outward demeanor may appear expressive and relational, but when people of these patterns are caught in their compulsion, their inner attitude is always impersonal. The Aggressive Stance is an offensive tactic that protects them from the world and other people. Usually they are well aware of their anger; they can express it to others, defining their limits and boundaries and even using it as a means to get their own way. However, in order to move as confidently as they do in the world, they must repress their fears—the fear of not being loved or of not succeeding, for example, as well as the natural caution that accompanies any difficult task.

Threes, Sevens, and Eights also share other qualities because of their common Repressed Relational Center. People of these patterns tend to be full of energy—optimistic go-getters. Task-oriented in their approach to life, they're always trying to get something going, to light a fire under others. Their eyes are fixed on the future, and because they feel things are moving too slowly, they impulsively keep stirring the pot of life and miss the pleasure of the present moment.

Most importantly, they appear to be impervious to feeling. Secretly afraid that if they express emotion it would overwhelm them and certain it would overwhelm others, they put feelings aside and lose themselves in activity.

The strength in this approach is that, if they choose, they can quickly dismiss personal offenses, remain optimistic, and prevent the negativity of one situation from contaminating another. In this way they are free to make creative and productive contributions to life. The weakness is that inattention to their interior lives and insensitivity to the needs and feelings of others keep them from developing the intimate relationships necessary to find personal fulfillment and meaning in life.

The Dependent Stance.   Ones, Twos, and Sixes are known as the dependent patterns. Looking to others to see what should happen next, they are social people who are constantly watching the reactions of those around them. They live this way because their need for acceptance is paramount. Wanting to be liked, thanked, and appreciated results in unstinting generosity, which is often accompanied by a subtle uneasiness that perhaps they've never really connected with the other person. What is missing in the Dependent Stance is the objectivity of "the big picture."

The reason these patterns become dependent in these ways is that they repress the Intellectual Center. The Intellectual Center thinks, plans, and remains objective; with it, people consider their life goals, plan how to attain them, and assess themselves and their place in the world. If you repress your ability to think for yourself, as these patterns do, the Dependent Stance is inevitable as you look to others for direction and validation.

By repressing their abilities to plan and work toward personal goals in the future, they allow the tyranny of the immediate to overtake them. They respond to the person, issue, or responsibility that faces them in the present moment without thinking through the consequences for their future. Then, feeling taken advantage of, they become resentful. By repressing the objective evaluation the Intellectual Center provides, they hold themselves hostage to the present moment and the opinions of others. Underneath an amiable exterior they can hold beliefs unsubstantiated by logic but demanding total loyalty; thus they have a tendency to be unforgiving when crossed.

Their outward demeanor may be socially adaptive and charming, but when they're caught in their compulsion, their inner attitude is always one of personal insecurity and need. The Dependent Stance protects them from ever having to look squarely at themselves. By placing too much importance on others and the world, they undervalue themselves. Disconcerted by the world and doubtful of their ability to deal with too much confusion, they can only take the world on its own terms each day. Relying heavily on their social connections to get through life means they must repress all feelings of anxiety about themselves as persons.

Ones, Twos, and Sixes also share other qualities because of their common Repressed Intellectual Center. People of high personal standards, they feel caught in a vise of tension as they attempt to meet the agendas others set for them according to these standards of performance. Feeling oppressed by the demands of the existing situation, they find it is not only difficult but almost impossible to grasp the big picture, especially in their personal lives.

Tenaciously attached to the project in front of them, if something that seems more important interrupts their connection, they may never get around to completing the original project. Most importantly, though they are opinionated about their values, they generally don't express their convictions directly.

The strength of this approach is a respect for others, a desire to interrelate rather than isolate, and an awareness of the importance of being responsible for living the basic moral values of a healthy society. The weakness is their need for others to affirm them because they can't affirm themselves. Recognizing and affirming personal strengths and talents would require the objectivity that only their Repressed Intellectual Center could provide.

The Withdrawing Stance. Fours, Fives, and Nines are known as the withdrawing patterns. Their inward focus and independent point of view is the result of their retreating into themselves and depending on their own strengths to get through life's difficulties. Interior people, they search for enlightened solutions to problems but, having come to a decision, may expect it to effect itself. Their commitment to protecting themselves and to their own values creates the force with which they expect to get through life. What is missing in the Withdrawing Stance is the confidence that they can make a difference in the world.

The reason these patterns become withdrawing in these ways is that they repress the Creative Center. This is the center of doing, spontaneity, and enthusiasm. By using it, people make things happen in their lives. Movement, resolve, and strategy proceed from this center, as do activity and effectiveness. If you repress your ability to act and accomplish things in your life and the world, as these patterns do, the Withdrawing Stance becomes the inevitable means of survival.

Feeling unable to affect other people or situations, they justify an exclusively interior approach to life. They retreat within themselves, thinking and feeling their way through life, devising enlightened solutions to problems while remaining detached from becoming personally involved. Because they believe they've processed information completely, they always consider themselves to be the final authority, regardless of what others might believe.

Their outward demeanor may be friendly and cooperative, but when caught in their compulsion, their inner attitude is always somewhat condescending. The Withdrawing Stance protects them from the world and people so that, like a castle surrounded by a moat and drawbridge, they can always detach themselves from the rest of the world. Their need for extreme self-protection proceeds from an inner anxiety about self and an uneasy feeling that others and the world are somewhat suspect. Because blind trust in people or the world is automatically out of the question, they rely completely on their own inner resources. Their lack of the self-confidence needed to deal realistically with the world and people leads to feelings of hostility and anger that they must continually repress in order to get along.

Fours, Fives, and Nines also share other qualities because of their common Repressed Creative Center. Their interior focus causes them to think about projects, plan them, and be aware of the feelings surrounding them, but they have a hard time actually getting them off the drawing board and beginning them. There always seems to be another detail to be thought through or feeling to process, and so they do much more thinking, feeling, or talking than actual doing. Deciding what they will do depends either on what they're interested in or whether there is an outside pressure being exerted on them. Everything else can justifiably remain in the planning stage. Familiarity with the world of mind and/or heart makes them experts at rationalizing their way out of difficult situations.

Most importantly, they cling to an individualistic direction because they are caught in the past. By pondering life and overanalyzing everything in an attempt to understand intricacies, they live the inner life as if it were life in the real world. Repressing the Creative Center has resulted in significant barriers that prevent them from freely entering into the world of productive activity.

The strength of this position is the ability to quickly perceive and comprehend the subtle complexities underlying complicated ideas or interpersonal associations. The weakness is that because their self-protective needs keep them separated from others and life, they miss experiencing the satisfaction of fulfillment found through personal relationship or creative, productive enterprise.

Repressed Center Is the Key

Looking at the nine patterns of the Enneagram from the point of view of Repressed Center, we come to an amazing discovery. The Repressed Center is the silent shadow in control of the personality. Because it is hidden in the unconscious, there are certain voids in our lives that must be filled by overusing and misusing other available strengths.

Repression, according to the dictionary, is the "process by which unacceptable desires or impulses are excluded from consciousness and left to operate in the unconscious." Realizing that we've repressed one third of the vital intelligence we need to live a healthy life, we are not surprised that other unhealthy attitudes must be developed to compensate for what has been excluded from consciousness.

One of the compensating attitudes we've described is the development of an Aggressive, Dependent, or Withdrawing approach to life. We relate to life in these ways to protect ourselves from having to deal with the parts of reality that we don't understand. In the process, we do develop certain wonderful strengths. Yet, when we look at the weaknesses that are also evident, we see that they are simply the exact opposite of the strengths. Thus, if we could access our Repressed Center, not only would those strengths and weakness be equalized, but a transcendent way of relating to reality would become available to us.

Another way of compensation is seen in the overuse of our Dominant Center of intelligence. We not only employ this intelligence in appropriate ways, but we exaggerate and distort it as a way of attempting to handle issues the Repressed Center is meant to handle—issues never meant to be within the Dominant Center's expertise. Again, we develop wonderful skills in our Dominant Center, while at the same time equal but opposite deficits or weaknesses are also appearing on the other side of the scale.

In the meantime, the shadow side, our unconscious Repressed Center that has been left behind to operate on its own, causes all kinds of disturbances in our lives. Like a child who feels ignored and becomes troublesome, it's continually trying to get our attention, as if shouting,

"Here I am!" "Hey, look! I'm still around!" "Notice me, or you'll be sorry!"

Let's look at a few of the ways our shadow creates havoc in our lives so that we will start paying attention. All the behaviors mentioned below will sneak out when we least expect them; because they feel uncontrollable at the time, we allow them to happen—even though we know that later we're going to have to clean up the mess we've made.

People who repress the Relational Center can in a moment become irritable, picky, and fault-finding. Intense seriousness about something of little consequence can overtake an otherwise delightful moment. Repressing feelings can also make them uncooperative, aloof, impulsively self-indulgent, or boisterous and overbearing in their attempt to be the center of attention.

People who repress the Intellectual Center can suddenly find themselves being extremely stubborn about some little thing. They can be opinionated, negative, rigid, sarcastic, jealous and domineering, or closed to any new ideas or suggestions.

People who repress the Creative Center can react suddenly and explosively to situations with no warning, and at other times be controlled by laziness. They can act irresponsibly, childishly, obstinately, or miserly, or they can start scheming and figuring out how to get even with someone who has crossed them.

The *coup de grace* is that the Repressed Center is not only controlling our lives but getting off scot-free whenever there is trouble, tension, or turmoil! Being repressed, it is virtually invisible, and so when these disruptive actions occur we don't know what to call to account inside us. We feel embarrassed by our behavior or we excuse it, but we don't see what corrective measures to take, because we rationalize our behavior as an isolated episode. Thus, our actions are repeated, and we continue trying to justify behavior that we don't even understand.

Humming Your Shadow Home

Now that we have noticed our shadow and understand that it's the forgotten part of ourselves, what do we do about it? Because we've banished it to live in the dark unconscious for so long, it's time to start inviting it back home—home to live in the light. For more than anything, our shadow longs to be embraced, needs to be held, healed, and loved back into life.

Maria José Hobday, an American Indian nun, says that among her native people there is a belief that when a child wakes up in the morning cranky and out of sorts, it is because during the night the child became separated from his or her shadow. The only solution, then, is for the child to be taken a good distance away from the family so that the child can "hum the shadow home." Unless that happens, the child will spread discontent among the whole family within a very short time.

Recounting a childhood experience when she woke up out of sorts, she relates how her father led her out into the grasslands near her home and told her that she could return to the family only after she hummed her shadow home. After her tears of humiliation and anger were spent, she began to hear the chirping of birds and the wind softly blowing through the grasses. Quiet now and listening, the little girl began to hum softly.

The shadow that this little Indian girl learned to cherish is very much like the Repressed Center. This intelligence has been consigned to the shadow land of the unconscious mind, there to be disruptive and unhelpful because it lies in darkness and is ignored. Focusing our attention on the other two-thirds of our minds—our Dominant and Support Centers—we divide ourselves and pit two parts of the mind against the other. From this internal struggle come our battles with ourselves, arguments with others, and failures at dealing with certain important aspects of life—those aspects that are the forte of the center we repress and do not use well.

"A house divided against itself cannot stand." Words of truth and wisdom such as these have a way of piercing through every level of a person's life. Whether applied to the world, a nation, a family, or an individual, the truth of this statement remains constant. Division begins in the lives of individuals and spreads its corruption through families, neighborhoods, and the whole of society. This reality is evident to anyone who picks up a newspaper, participates in a contentious meeting, or feels anxiety grow while walking through a dark parking lot or waiting alone at night to catch the bus.

We are seldom aware, however, that when unity begins in the lives of individuals it has an even greater power to spread through families, neighborhoods, and the whole of society. Few of us believe that our personal efforts each day to be more conscious and loving are going to make much difference in the whole scheme of life. Yet, all of us have heard stories of how one person or a few good people changed the whole course of someone's life and led that person to make great contributions to the betterment of society. Because of one kind act or one loving gesture, or through a quiet life of gentle responsiveness, thousands of lives can be changed for the better by someone whose face or name will be remembered for only a short time by a few people.

Could José Hobday's father ever have imagined the positive impact that his actions that day long ago would have, not only in the life of his daughter, but in the lives of the thousands that would hear her story? Can any of us comprehend how the small act of love expressed today has the potential of affecting thousands? And if we were able to catch a glimpse of the possible effects that our actions today would have on others, would we live and love differently?

The concern for humanity, according to the age-old wisdom of the Enneagram, is that people fail to apply the three kinds of intelligence in a healthy, unified manner in daily life. The task in life is to *wake up* and become aware of how the imbalanced use of intelligence not only divides us internally but also becomes the cause of division and destruction in relationships and in the world.

Unity internally and externally is the goal, the aim, the purpose of this wisdom. Instead of overusing two centers—the Dominant and Support Centers—we must learn to use all three centers, each for the purpose for which it is created. Then, as the Enneagram Riddle (see the Introduction) says, *two become three.*

Therefore, unless we become aware of how we are out of balance—divided within—we cannot see and understand how we are a negative force in the world. Once the imbalance is recognized, however, we are able to begin making positive choices that will lead to unity and freedom.

How we think, feel, and act today is creating the future. The future—yours, ours, society's—is being shaped this very moment. What will happen depends entirely upon how we live and what we desire in our ordinary, day to day lives. At this very moment we are creating the future—ours, our children's, and our children's children's for generations to come.

In this context, learning to "hum our shadow home" takes on new significance. Bringing our three centers into harmonic resonance is the language of love and unity that heals the individual soul and the soul of the world.

When we were young, we may have been "humming our shadow home" without even realizing we were doing so. Taking time under an old tree, wandering in the fields or forests, or simply retreating to a quiet place in our home, we found a way to think through our fears, comfort our hurts, let our imaginations roam free, and come to know once more the joy of living as we again became centered, balanced, in harmony.

Years have passed since we intuitively understood the wisdom of taking time to hum our shadows home. Because we live in a culture so filled with noise that it demands all our attention, the power of being outdoors and humming in solitude—in harmony with the music of nature and the rhythm of the earth—may be as critical to human survival as food and water.

We have been separated from our Repressed Center—our shadow—for too long. Isn't it time to love ourselves and others enough to hum our shadows home?

For Personal and Group Work

1. Everyone has a Dominant, Support, and Repressed Center. No matter what type you are, you could say that your compulsive personality pattern is composed as follows: qualities from your Dominant Center are 55 percent of your personality; from your Support Center, 40 percent; and from your Repressed Center, 5 percent. Identify your Dominant, Support, and Repressed Centers and the ways you express each. How does your personality and lifestyle reflect this formula?

2. Understanding the effect of repressing one center of intelligence is key to transformation and growth. The absence of the positive qualities of your Repressed Center will be most obvious in your personal life, because we learn what we need to learn to perform our job well, whether we do it at home or in the marketplace. What are the qualities from your Repressed Center that you see lacking in your everyday life? What have been the consequences of not having these qualities available in your relationships? In your daily activities? In your life goals?

3. If you're going to hum your shadow home, you need first to identify times, places, and activities that will stave off the responsibilities of daily life for a while so you can be at home with yourself. This can only happen if you follow these steps:

a. Name the activities you can do alone that bring you inner calm and peace.

b. Name the places you need to find or get to that will allow you the quiet for these activities.

c. Figure out the minimal amount of time you would need for each of these activities.

d. Look at your schedule and find the time do to them. If you say there is no time, look again. If you still can't see your way clear to finding time for yourself, talk to another person about this issue, for example, a trusted friend, a counselor, a clergy person, or someone you recognize already knows how to clear time in his or her schedule for inner work. Allow this person to guide you through the process of reworking your own schedule.

4. All of us have areas in our lives in which we have become rigid and inflexible—politics, religion, family values and expectations, friendships, and others. Can you identify a rigid and inflexible area in your life? Do you know why this particular area is rigid? Would you consider trying to perceive beneath the surface of that rigid belief system to see if there is another ever-changing dimension of truth that might become visible to you?

5

The Hidden Wound

―――――

If we could read the secret history of our "enemies," we should find in each man and woman's life sorrow enough to disarm all hostility.
—HENRY WADSWORTH LONGFELLOW

Have you ever wondered who you *really* are?" "Do you ever think about why you are on this earth?" "Who do you think you were created to be?" "What do *you* believe?"

Years ago someone asked a friend of ours these questions. At the time she found them both foolish and irritating. "I'd worked hard all my life to be a good, responsible member of society," she recounted. "In my mind, the only people who could afford to waste time on questions like those were either cloistered monks and nuns, the very rich, or people attempting to justify their own irresponsible behavior." Because she strongly believed that her friend was justifying irresponsibility and said so, any desire to venture into a philosophical discussion was quickly replaced by an intense interest in a safer, if more mundane, topic.

A few years later, after a series of severe emotional and financial losses, this good, responsible woman could only watch helplessly as her carefully constructed life tumbled down around her. In the beginning she thought she was strong enough to handle even these devastating blows, but as her life grew progressively worse, even the wish to go on living began slipping away.

"In a moment of near despair," she recalled, "those silly questions began to drift through my mind, bringing the first flicker of light I'd seen in what seemed like an eternity. Because I had nothing left to lose, I began trying to respond to them as honestly as I could."

Today, nearly ten years later, she is utterly convinced that the falling apart of her life was a great blessing and the questions she had been so quick to reject were gifts from God.

"They were Sacred Questions—but I was so blind I couldn't see the light in them until my life became as black as a moonless night." With a wry smile she added, "Without those 'foolish' questions I might have lived my whole life never knowing the difference between existing and being *alive*. It's the difference between living in a two-dimensional and a three-dimensional world."

The experience she describes, although unique to her, contains the unbroken threads of the great mythic patterns that have been woven through every generation since the beginning of time. The mythologist Joseph Campbell described this common human story when he said that "at the bottom of the abyss comes the voice of salvation. The black moment is the moment when the real message of transformation is going to come. At the darkest moment comes the light."[1]

No matter how varied the circumstances may appear, stories of life, death, and rebirth always speak of a journey into the deep and silent recesses of self. It takes great courage to sit alone in this shadowy silence, sorting and sifting through our lives in an attempt to awaken personal conscience and touch what is true for us. On this quest we find that truth, like understanding, can never be stagnant. It's either growing or dying, evolving or devolving. Perhaps Jung communicated this idea most simply and profoundly: "All true things must change and only that which changes remains true."[2]

Many people believe that by focusing on facts they can be confident of the truth they proclaim. They simply dismiss the reality that *feelings are also facts*. Likewise, people who exaggerate the importance of feelings as irrefutable facts easily dismiss the validity of external reality. Both perceptions lack substance and balance. Unless we go through the hard work of soul making and awakening personal conscience, external facts remain the same, feelings remain fickle and egocentric, perceptions of truth become rigid and judgmental, hearts shrivel, and we lead isolated, meaningless lives.

---

[1] Joseph Campbell, *The Power of Myth* (New York: Doubleday, 1988), p. 39.

[2] "The Nature and Activity of the Psyche," in *The Collected Works of C. G. Jung*, Bollingen Series 20, vol. 14 (Princeton, NJ: Princeton Univ. Press, 1969), par. 503.

One of the most disorienting aspects of unearthing what is true, alive, and changing is that many familiar, accepted, and safe ideas of right and wrong, good and evil begin to slip through our fingers. Because they have no life apart from that which we have given them, they decay into dust, and we are left with a void, an emptiness that appears impossible to fill.

Concepts and images of God that we had unquestioningly accepted since childhood begin to crumble, and now we question whether we have any faith at all or if we even know what faith is. Or who God is. Or *if* God is.

Our lives are no longer neatly packaged or clearly mapped out with a destination plainly in view. There is only a vague, uncertain sense of direction, and though we don't understand, we believe, we doubt, we struggle, we question, and we believe once again.

And in the questioning faith is born. And hope. And compassion. And we are born as, in this land of shadows and light, every painful scar of our life is woven into a single membrane—a wildly beautiful wounded womb where a real beautiful self sleeps and where God lives, waiting to breathe new life into us. In this holy place called *soul,* healing begins seeping slowly into the parched earth of our being.

Into the Wound

In describing nine compulsive personality types, and in declaring that the origins of compulsive personality lie

in the imbalanced and improper use of the three intelligences, the Enneagram first points out what is wrong
in our lives. But it does not do so in a judgmental way,
for what could be the origin of such a maladaptive approach to life but a wound to the personality, a wound
so significant and basic that it becomes the primary formative experience in our lives? In uncovering this Original wound, we will discover the pain that frightens us
away from the inner land of soul into the outer world of
compulsion.

What is our Original Wound, and what is its origin?
Our earliest life experience tells the tale. For each person,
the story is unique and different, supremely personal. It
is the story of our conception and birth, our infancy and
childhood, our parents and/or other care givers, our education both formal and informal, and our choices.

Yet for each of us the story is also the same: we were
created good, born into a flawed and egocentric world,
expressed our truest self, and found our essential self did
not satisfy or meet the needs of those into whose lives we
were born. Their flawed natures touched us, not necessarily out of malice—although unfortunately that can be
the case as well—but more often out of their human need
and limited perspectives. Even doing their best, no parent, no care giver can respond to an infant or a child in
precisely the way that little one needs at every moment.

Personality is created out of the interplay between an
infant who brings into this world a "native endowment,"
for example, tendencies, interests, and genetically hard-
wired talents and deficiencies, and the nurturing envi-

ronment, the people, situations, opportunities, and limitations into whose circle the child is born.[3] Into that interplay come many obstructions and problems—some originating in care givers and others coming from impersonal sources—and the child responds to them as well as he or she can.

It is not just the experiences a child has, however, that make the difference. Even more important is the way in which the child takes those experiences into him- or herself. Why would a child, who is created with all three centers equal and in balance and ready to accomplish the task for which it is created, repress one center at some point before the age of five?[4]

The only answer can be that through childhood experience the person comes to associate danger, loss of love, and/or lack of fulfillment of basic needs with that center. *The unconscious motivation of each Enneagram pattern is the direct result of this Original Wound.*

The Original Wound within each of us, then, is carried by a child who wears our face. Where else could we look for this child who has been imprisoned all these years but in the hidden shadow land of our personality that we have come to know as our Repressed Center?

---

[3]For example, see *The Psychological Birth of the Human Infant,* by Margaret Mahler, Fred Pine, and Anni Bergman (New York: Basic Books, 1975).

[4]The best psychological research has shown how personality structure is set in place by the age of five. See Mahler et al., *The Psychological Birth of the Human Infant,* for detailed research and commonly accepted theory in this field.

Wounds in the Repressed Relational Center

Why do Threes, Sevens, and Eights repress the Relational Center? Why do they undervalue emotions, relationships, and personal needs, sacrificing them to the gods of activity, accomplishment, and image? Somewhere in their earliest months or years, perhaps even in the womb, they experienced something that they took in as relational alienation or separation and deep emotional pain.[5]

People who have attended our seminars have reported a number of examples of what causes these wounds in the womb or the very early years: Parents wanting a boy may have a girl. A mother may be feeling grief at the death of a parent during pregnancy or the child's early infancy. A child may be separated from mother and/or father in early infancy because of the child's or a parent's severe illness. A parent may be emotionally absent because of alcoholism or workaholism, and the other parent may consequently dominate (positively or negatively) the child's life. The child may have been given up for adoption. A parent may be insensitive or unable to respond to the child's emotional needs.

Whatever the specific experience, the child's reaction was to reject the Relational Center, to reject emotions

---

[5]The idea that people have formative and memorable experiences in the womb is an old one that is now being corroborated by research. See, for example, *The Secret Life of the Unborn Child,* by Thomas Verny, M.D., and John Kelly (New York: Dell, 1981).

and relationships, to reject intimacy. Remember: it's not the exact experience that matters so much as the way the child absorbed it. Because they reacted to the experience in terms of emotions and relationships, *their ability to feel love was wounded.* Thus, their greatest challenges and struggles in life will be in *becoming vulnerable to intimate relationships.*

If your freedom to love yourself was wounded, you became an Eight.   Inwardly, Eights are hardest on themselves; thus, they feel justified in treating other people and life the same way they treat themselves—with power and strength. They impose a savior complex on themselves, feeling if they don't fight for justice, no one else will. They find introspection difficult because they don't like what they find when they look within. If you find self-love difficult, you must keep up a show of strength lest anyone find out how vulnerable you really are and take advantage of you.

Eights' lifelong struggle with feeling unimportant, combined with the pain of feeling unworthy of their own personal attention and love, demands that they live in the external world of activity.[6] The wound that has curtailed their freedom to believe that they are important enough to be loved or cared for personally is unconsciously reflected in the way they use their power in the world to prove their importance.

---

[6]The lifelong struggle given here for each of the types is associated with their Preferred Centers, which are described in chapter 2.

Refusing to allow others to treat them as insignificant—which is how they treat themselves—they become champions of justice who protect their own rights and the rights of others whom society treats as insignificant or unimportant. By repressing emotional sensitivity to themselves, they summon the toughness needed to withstand the sting of dealing with a recalcitrant world. Using their strength and energy to command respect and truth in the outer world is the way they have learned to deal with their unconscious pain of feeling unworthy of being loved.

If your freedom to love others was wounded, you became a Seven. Sevens use their agile minds to keep people at bay. With a flurry of ideas, words, and activity they run helter-skelter through life, looking for the pleasure that will fill the void of having no one to love. That is why, when they do find someone they can connect with, they become totally dedicated to that relationship. If you find loving others difficult, it's best at least to keep them laughing and happy so that you can get along and make the best of a painful situation.

Sevens' lifelong struggle with feeling incapable, combined with the pain of feeling unable to love others adequately, demands that they do the next best thing and just try to make life happy. Needing to keep life and people always feeling good confines them to the internal world of ideas and planning, where the reality of pain can be avoided.

They unconsciously express their inability to love others in their efforts to keep a constantly optimistic attitude and in their multiple lighthearted relationships. They use their mental agility to devise solutions for other people's problems but never dare to risk personal involvement in enacting those solutions for fear they'll be proven incapable. With their unconscious longing to love others unfulfilled, they feel lonely, and their gluttonous desire for pleasure becomes the only escape from an interior desert.

If your freedom to love yourself and others was wounded, you became a Three.   Threes get caught in the tension of trying to balance their inner and outer worlds and lose themselves in the process. Aware of feelings in both self and others because their Preferred Center is the Relational Center, they live midway between the inner world of focusing on goals and the outer world of activity. Their variety of interests creates the illusion of being a well-rounded person, while in fact it distracts them from going deeper into life and discovering the true meaning of their existence. If you find loving others or yourself difficult, you'd better do as much as you can and create the illusion of success, but never expect yourself, others, or life to be real, deep, or satisfying.

Threes' lifelong struggle with feeling unlovable, combined with the pain of feeling incapable of loving self or others, demands they live on the razor's edge between worlds—dipping into their inner world and into relationships, dipping into ideas and into activity, committing themselves to none and therefore finding no lasting happiness. The wound that has diminished their freedom to believe they are able to give or receive love is unconsciously reflected in their attempts to balance a multiplicity of interests that distract others from focusing on them as a person.

Feeling unlovable, they avoid revealing any personal deficiencies lest they give anyone an opportunity to affirm what they already believe to be true. They deceive themselves by focusing their inner life on devising plans and setting goals, which prevents the pain of feeling unlovable from surfacing. Through success and a charming image, they establish the many friendly associations that become substitutes for intimacy. This deception yields the only replacement—admiration—that alleviates their unconscious pain of feeling worthless and unable to love others.

Summary.   Threes, Sevens, and Eights compensate for the loss of love by looking to the future and by being optimistic. You can't love what doesn't yet exist, and you don't have to love what might someday be wonderful and fantastically successful.

Wounds in the Repressed Intellectual Center

Why do Ones, Twos, and Sixes repress the Intellectual Center? Why do they undervalue the trustworthiness of information about themselves, of the perspective you can gain by looking at the big picture, or of their own or other people's opinions? Somewhere in their earliest months or years, perhaps even in the womb, they experienced something that gave them a feeling of unreliability regarding their world and/or themselves.

These are some examples from people who have attended our seminars: being given minimal physical care as an infant; being told "I love you" but experiencing violence or abuse contradicting that message; having parents whose emotional volatility made the child's world unstable; being seen as a substitute for another child who had recently died or separated from the family; being treated as a substitute for the opposite sex child that was really wanted—a boy might have been referred to in degrading feminine terms, a girl treated as if she were just one of the guys, or a child of either sex expected to be responsible for situations that called for maturity beyond his or her years.

Whatever the specific experience, these children's reaction was to reject the Intellectual Center, to reject the trustworthiness of what they were told or of what they thought, to reject their ability to perceive reality accurately. Remember: it's not the exact experience that matters so much as the way the child digested it. Because these children saw the experience in terms of information, ideas, and opinions, *their ability to feel trust was wounded.* Thus, their greatest challenges and struggles in life will be in *learning to give and receive trust.*

If your freedom to trust yourself was wounded, you became a Two. Inwardly, Twos don't trust their own thoughts or feelings. That is why they are trying to earn everyone else's trust by helping them. They don't look within themselves, because whatever they find there has no value to them. They usually don't know what they want aside from other people's wishes or preferences, even when pressed for a response. If you don't trust yourself, you had best rely on others' needs, feelings, and preferences to set your agenda.

Twos' lifelong struggle with feeling unlovable, combined with the pain of feeling they can't trust the information coming from inside them, demands they flee into other people's worlds. The wound that causes them not to trust the inner information of their own thoughts, feelings, needs, and desires is reflected in the ways they are solicitous of everyone else's. Unable to find guidance from within, they seek it from everyone else; other people's needs actually become their own.

Feeling unworthy of love reinforces this outward thrust as they seek to escape the many reasons they feel undeserving of attention and affection. Refusing to allow others to mistrust them—because that is the way they treat themselves—they create dependent relationships that elicit others' trust with their self-effacing demeanor, their concern for them, and their seemingly limitless ability to put aside their own needs for the sake of others. Taking the slightly superior attitude of meeting others' needs but refusing to admit their own is the way they've learned to deal with their unconscious and unfulfilled longing to trust themselves.

If your freedom to trust others was wounded, you became a One.   Ones set extraordinarily high standards for themselves and then are secretly disappointed when others' standards are not as perfectionistic. Their mistrust of others causes them to draw inward, depend on themselves, and take an overresponsible attitude in an effort to create something good in what feels like an unmanageable world. Their desire to trust others sometimes takes the form of flinging caution to the wind and giving up control of the situation, but they usually feel they pay the price when others take advantage of them. If you don't trust others, you have to rely on yourself alone to get the job done right.

Ones' lifelong struggle with feeling unimportant, combined with the pain of feeling they can't count on others to be there for them, demands that they intensify their own response to life in order to make a difference. By continually monitoring their response, they refine it until it is perfected in their own eyes; in this way they achieve some semblance of self-importance, at least for a while.

They unconsciously express their inability to trust others in the way they play their emotional cards close to their vest, and by their solitary approach to work, which ensures that their own standards will govern the outcome. Compliments are difficult for them to receive, both because their basic feeling is that they are personally insignificant and because they believe others aren't expert enough in the field to be able to make an accurate judgment. With their unconscious desire to trust others unfulfilled, they learn to resent a world that forces them to make up for its untrustworthiness with their own intensity and serious response to life.

If your freedom to trust yourself and others was wounded, you became a Six. Sixes feel insecure and need to be reassured constantly that they are accepted, welcomed, and appreciated. One person's affirmation isn't enough, two affirmations aren't enough, ten aren't enough; and when they are enough for today, tomorrow we start all over again. Sixes are caught in the need to balance inner and outer reality, which they perceive in terms of their Preferred Intellectual Center. Thus, though they are aware of their own evaluations and other people's, they trust neither and continue to seek the security of 100 percent corroboration; yet, after they gather mountains of verification, they still feel uneasy when they make a decision. If you can't completely trust yourself or others, you had best gather around yourself as many tokens of affirmation and security as possible so that you can keep your worst fear at bay.

Sixes' lifelong struggle with feeling incapable, combined with their inability to trust self or others, creates an ever-changing environment. They walk between worlds of thoughts and feelings, relationships, activities, and responsibilities because each holds an unfulfilled promise of happiness. They dip into each of these worlds but can't feel safe or secure about committing to any of them; therefore, true inner peace eludes them.

The wound that cripples their ability to trust self or others is unconsciously expressed in their continual need for reassurance, which they often perceive as being relational. Through many social relationships they create a network of support systems that take the edge off the gnawing feeling that nothing in this world can be counted on. Being responsible is their attempt to disprove their own inner feelings of incompetency and powerlessness. Continual wariness and vague anxiety about life feel like the only rational response to an untrustworthy world.

Summary.   Ones, Twos, and Sixes compensate for the loss of trust by focusing on the present moment and by being myopic. You don't need faith when you live only in the present moment, and a myopic perspective focuses on hard facts that eliminate the need for trust.

Wounds in the Repressed Creative Center

Why do Fours, Fives, and Nines repress the Creative Center? Why do they undervalue their own ability to make their mark on the world, to respond confidently to life, to effect change in the important areas of life? Their earliest months or years, including their months in the womb, were marked by an experience that gave them a feeling of hopelessness about their world and/or themselves.

These are some examples from people who have attended our seminars: being the child of two parents who did not love each other, or of parents who both had a repressed or secondary Relational Center; having many different caretakers in the earliest months of life; being an unwanted child; having one or both parents severely depressed or mentally ill during the child's infancy; being adopted after weeks or months as an orphan.

Whatever the specific experience, the children's reaction was to reject the Creative Center, to reject their ability to make a difference to others, thereby discounting their own inner strength. Remember: it is not the exact experience that matters so much as the way the child assimilated it. Because these people saw the experience in terms of actions that affected their safety, *their ability to feel hope was wounded*. Thus, their greatest challenges and struggles in life will be in *learning to hope and to imagine a future filled with hope*.

If your freedom to hope in yourself was wounded, you became a Five.   Fives mask the inner emptiness they feel as persons by depersonalizing themselves and all of life, reducing it to information. They pull back from social and personal relationships and want or allow someone else—often their spouse—to handle these situations for them. If you can't find in yourself a reason to hope for a better future, you had best rely on someone else to be your future while you retreat into an ivory tower of ideas.

Fives' lifelong struggle with feeling incapable, combined with the pain of feeling unworthy of their own confidence in themselves, demands they become experts in the world of outside knowledge. Here they can occupy their time and energy with the laudable goal of gaining wisdom while avoiding their inner pangs of emptiness. The wound that has reduced their ability to feel confident in themselves is unconsciously reflected in the way they plan a project or gather information but never feel quite ready to execute the project or share their wisdom with others.

Secretly desiring and needing others to express confidence in them because they can't feel it for themselves, they take the slightly superior and condescending role of expert to cover their feelings of incapability. Becoming greedy for outside information, knowledge, theories, and ideas is the way they've learned to deal with the unconscious pain of feeling they can't rely on themselves personally.

If your freedom to hope in others was wounded, you became a Four. Fours are obsessed with self-inventory, because they feel everything depends on them. Inwardly certain that no one else cares about them or values them as human beings, they create the attention they need by being different, dramatic, and self-praising. Both their intense awareness of their feelings and the need to express them proceed from the sense that, unless they are heard and understood, they will get lost in the shuffle. If you can't find a reason to hope in others, you had best take care of your own needs first; maybe then you'll be able to get by in this world.

Fours' lifelong struggle with feeling unlovable, combined with the pain of not being able to rely on others, confines them to their own interior world, where they convince themselves that, if they search long enough and deep enough, they will find the gift or talent that will make their life worthwhile. Propelled in this intense inner search by the fear that they are insignificant, they over-compensate for their inferior feelings with a superior attitude.

They unconsciously express their inability to depend on others by testing the strength of their friendships, often to the point of breaking, and by drawing attention to their gifts, which they simultaneously demean. As they express the depth of their feelings for others, they unconsciously manipulate them to express their feelings in return, attempting to stave off the fear that they are unworthy of the relationship altogether. Envious feelings inevitably invade the emptiness created by their unconscious and unfulfilled longing to hope in others.

If your freedom to hope in yourself and others was wounded, you became a Nine.   Nines feel little self-esteem and get along by being affable but impersonal. Because they prefer the Creative Center and thus are aware of their own and others' power, Nines feel caught in the need to balance inner and outer pressure. They resist the inward psychological and spiritual journey, while outwardly they are unaware that their words or actions make any difference to others or that they are significant to others. If you are hopeless about yourself and others, you had best remain unaware of important issues and keep up a lighthearted exterior.

Nines' lifelong struggle with feeling unimportant, combined with the pain of not being able to depend on self or others, forces them to live in the lonely land of inactivity, except for having fun. They fear that in exerting themselves to make a difference they will only be proven as unimportant; they can't believe they can ever be personally significant to another person.

The wound that has decreased their ability to depend on self or others is unconsciously reflected in the way they avoid arguments, problems, and personal responsibilities—anything that would call forth stamina in the personal realm—as well as in their preoccupation with impersonal activities like problem solving, research, and intellectual pursuits. They've learned to deal with their unconscious and unfulfilled longing to hope in themselves and others by choosing to ignore the serious side of life and instead living a playful and carefree existence.

Summary. Fours, Fives, and Nines compensate for the loss of hope by focusing on the past and by being pessimistic. You don't need to hope for something that has already happened, or if you remain focused on the faults, problems, and stumbling blocks you are likely to encounter.

Wounding and Healing: Personal and Global

Everything of the past
and everything of the present
and everything of the future

God creates
in the innermost realms of the human soul.
—MEISTER ECKHART

As we are drawn toward the millennium, it is becoming more and more important that we become soul makers and healers, because the spread of violence and disease is accelerating at an unbelievably rapid rate. The lost feminine qualities and values need to be freed from exile, because these are the qualities that nurture, heal, regenerate, and unite what has been divided. Integrating and synthesizing feminine awareness and the Divine Feminine into our consciousness will counteract violence. The wounded child within each of us is the vessel containing the lost feminine.

The first step is to embrace the pain we have carried within and to feel compassion for our wounded inner selves. In this way we awaken, receive divine grace, and stir the waters of healing that flow in the deep and holy places within.

Because of the Original Wound we became divided in our thinking, feeling, and doing. Thus we, too, banished the feminine by leaving our wounded child—our real beautiful self—untended. This inner child, who wears the face of personal and collective pain and therefore was exiled from our consciousness, has been cared for by the God who lives within the secret sanctuary of our soul, for God will always be found in the place we are most in need.

The wounding and exile of our inner child—no matter how it happened—resulted in a division within our psyche; therefore, we became dualistic in the entire way we live our lives. We've become conditioned to interpreting life as an either-or proposition, and we have lost touch with the ability to span divisions with a both-and attitude. Only by reclaiming and uniting with that lost part of ourselves can we experience the healing we long for.

How have we, as individuals, been impoverished because of the effects of our Original Wound? Each of us has had our freedom to access one of the three great virtues—faith, hope, love—severely restricted. Each one of these virtues connects us to ourselves, others, God, and the universe in vital, life-giving ways.

It's as if the Original Wound began a process of corrosion on a vital connection in our internal circuitry. Throughout our lives that initial experience of pain has drawn similar experiences to itself over and over. Even though all our internal wiring is good, the corrosion grows over time. Although a small amount of current or power has continued to flow through that terminal, it needs some attention and repair. What is the source of the power whose flow has diminished during the course of our lives? It is the forgotten child who lives within us!

Those who carry the pain of betrayal (Ones, Twos, and Sixes), because of a corroded connection to their Repressed Intellectual Center, have a short circuit that restricts the power flow needed to activate the virtue of faith. They have had myriad experiences of searching for a place they belonged, a place they fit in, only to have trusted friends or family betray them once again. In whom do they dare to place their faith?

Those who carry the pain of abandonment (Fours, Fives, and Nines), because of a corroded connection to their Repressed Creative Center, have a short circuit that restricts the power flow needed to activate the virtue of hope. They have continually struggled with experiences of being rejected, of being left behind by someone they cared about. In whom do they dare to place their hope?

Those who carry the pain of estrangement (Threes, Sevens, and Eights), because of a corroded connection to their Repressed Relational Center, have a short circuit that restricts the power flow needed to activate the virtue of love. They have had countless episodes of people they love suddenly turning on them, using them, or inexplicably separating from them either emotionally and/or physically. To whom do they dare give their love?

Paul of Tarsus said there are three things that last: faith, hope, and love. In one spiritual tradition these are called the "theological virtues," from the Greek *theos* and *logos,* the "understanding of God," and the Latin *virtus,* "strength" or "power." Faith, hope, and love are the three power connections between heaven and earth that will enlighten and unite a divided universe. Unity with the divine gives life meaning, purpose, value.

The spiritual hunger that is gnawing in the depths of society today—activated by an outpouring of divine grace—is drawing us into the holy place within where healing and spirituality will be reborn. The signs that grace is alive and permeating the whole of creation are everywhere. For grace, you see, is not a thing. The materialistic West creates a desire to possess, turning even spiritual realities into things. Rather, the truth is that people *are graced,* creation *is graced.* Grace is a mode of being, and it enters this world relationally. It's like being loved. The experience of being loved doesn't give me anything new—it makes me a new person. Further, it's a gift, completely unmerited, completely free.

In Greek, the word *grace* is *charis* (pronounced KAR-is), and its first meaning comes from the language of art and the language of relationship. *Charis* is loveliness, beauty, outward grace; a gratification, a delight; gratitude; a kindness, a favor done; an offering, a gift. Thus, grace is God's loveliness shining on the earth, God's smiling on human beings. It's God making the world fresh and beautiful again, God gifting human beings with beauty. It creates friendship and the bond of friendship, gratitude.

Our task is to welcome grace and allow it to strengthen us on the journey into the world of our own soul so that we can return and revitalize the soul of the world. We are fast approaching the crossroads of the millennium. Will there ever be a better time to allow the light of Sacred Questions to rise up within us and to rise up within society? If not today, when?

Perhaps the reason we so often fail to recognize Sacred Questions when they rise up is that we're afraid that if we follow them we'll lose control and be hurt once again. Perhaps we fear to wonder who we really are, to think about why we are on this earth, or to question what we really believe. Yet, if we do choose to allow the light in these Sacred Questions to guide us into the land of soul, we will meet the God who lives within, the God who has been caring for our wounded child, and we will be united with what has been lost. And from a soul womb woven from the pain in our life, faith will be born, hope will be born, love will be born—and we will be reborn.

From Healing the Soul to Healing the Earth

The recognition that there is an Original Wound, a genesis of pain, is nothing new. Today, more than ever before—in fields as diverse as medical research, religion, the physical sciences, and psychology, to name a few—humanity is attempting to discover the origins of everything. To understand what went wrong is to obtain insights that can guide us toward healing.

In a television interview about the 1990 PBS series on the American Civil War, one of the authors, Ken Burns, described the Civil War as "the great trauma of our childhood as a nation." He said that, when his team began research into that period of history, they never expected to discover what they actually found. What they realized was that America had experienced one great wound; that out of that wound were born great weaknesses and great strengths; and that "we the people" continue to bear that wound, with all its strengths and weaknesses, even today.

No one in the world today could look at his or her own nation, or any nation in the world, and not strongly suspect that every land has experienced a great wound, a great trauma at some time in its history. No one could look at the earth being ravaged and laid waste by greed and not realize that the earth, too, has had a great wound inflicted on her.

From the beginning of time, the earth has undergone the shattering trauma of the collective wounding of all the nations and peoples who have called her home. She has received the pain of frightened young men and women as their lifeblood soaked into her breast. She has listened as the hungry cries of children, relentlessly piercing her heart day and night, went unheeded by all except a few. She has honored the bones of the innocent and the guilty alike, enfolding them in the sacred silence of her bosom. She has waited through the deep stillness of eternal nights for tears of the old, the sick, and the lonely to spill softly to the ground and mingle with her own—all the while feeling another part of her beautiful countenance being destroyed by exploding bombs.

Some who read this may not understand that we are describing a dimension of reality that lies just beyond and beneath the surface of the physical dimension of reality we are so familiar with. The global implications of this hidden realm of reality broke through to us in a new way just over a decade ago when we were presenters at a conference being held in one of the Southern states.

We had never visited this part of the country before and so were looking forward to the plans we had made to take a few days off after the conference and explore the area. I (Kathy) was staying with a couple who lived close to the conference site. After the evening sessions I would take a shortcut to their home by walking across a large open field. The spring nights were warm, the conference was going well, and the air was filled with the fragrance of flowers and blossoming trees. I was feeling relaxed and happy walking home that first evening.

Suddenly I felt as if the ground moved. I stood still, a little frightened and wondering if earthquakes were frequent in this part of the country. Everything was still, so I decided that my imagination must have been playing tricks on me, and I started to walk again. I had only gone a few feet when the ground beneath me moved again. It almost felt like a rolling movement.

I stood perfectly still and hardly breathing while everything in me stayed totally alert—watching, listening. I began to hear what seemed like the soft, convulsive breathing of a child who has been crying for a long time. Then, as I heard one deeper convulsive intake of breath, the ground moved again, and I dropped to my knees, listening. It seemed as if the earth was weeping.

The whole experience couldn't have lasted more than five or ten minutes. When I stood up and continued on my way, everything seemed perfectly normal again. By the time I arrived at my destination I had convinced myself that it was simply an aberration—that I had been so relaxed my imagination had just taken off on its own. I put it out of my mind and never mentioned the incident to anyone.

The next evening the incident was repeated and, with only slight variations, continued every evening that week. I told no one until the final morning of the conference when, somewhat timid and more than a little embarrassed, I approached our host and began to explain what had been happening to me. Gratefully, he listened without interrupting and showed no signs of disbelief or skepticism. When I finished he said, "Since you're planning to spend a few days in the area, I would like to take you on a tour of the countryside tomorrow morning. Perhaps then you'll understand why I find nothing unusual about what you've just told me."

The next day we saw a land that had been ravaged by chemical waste. We heard of the high numbers of people in that area who had died from "unusual" forms of cancer and of the unaccountably high numbers of stillborn babies and babies born with physical deformities. Two months later, the woman whose home I stayed in during that week died of one of those unusual forms of cancer. Yes, we know the earth weeps—and God weeps.

Who will heal this earth that convulses in agony if not us? Who will heal the peoples of the earth if not us? Who will heal the wounded nations if not us? Who will heal the children if not us? Where will the healing that can permeate society, the earth, the universe begin except within each one of us?

On the surface it appears selfish to look at all the wounds of the world and then focus back on oneself. Yet, until we can hear the cries of the wounded child within us, our ears will be closed to the cries of the children of the earth. Until we can touch and kiss and heal our own wounds, we will continue to tear open the wounds of others. In asking the Sacred Questions that draw us near to our own Original Wound, we expand our awareness so that in our presence others can be themselves. In becoming soul makers, we become healers. In becoming healers we become co-creators with God of our own destiny and the destiny of the world.

For Personal and Group Work

1. Life has a way of shifting our perspective with time. Some experiences that at first seemed filled with possibility became dead-end streets; other experiences that at first were devastating finally yielded great reward. Can you recall a time in your life when something that appeared to be a tragedy was in retrospect a gift? Describe your experience, your feelings, and your interpretation.

2. Every type in the Enneagram has a unique Original Wound. Identify your Original Wound and reread the description of it. Write down the aspects of the wound that apply to you with several lines of space after each; underline or mark with an asterisk those aspects that stand out as particularly important. Repeat the word or phrase you've written, and after each repetition write down the association that comes to your mind. In this way you will be writing down your personal associations with each aspect of your wound.

When you are finished writing your associations, look at all you've written to see if there is a memory or series of stories associated with that part of your life. Write these stories in your journal or tell those stories to a trusted friend.

3. Often the stories you associate with your Original Wound reveal a pattern of behavior or experience in your life. Look at your stories from this perspective and discern the underlying pattern(s) in them. How can you use your insights from the repeating patterns of your Original Wound to make more conscious, intentional, and constructive choices for your life?

4. As you look to healing the Original Wound in your life, explore the various avenues available to you for healing—for example, counseling, spiritual direction, prayer, meditation, group work. Which of these avenues attracts you, and how can you employ these means in the process of healing the Original Wound and reclaiming your inner child?

6

Remembering Our Destiny

I, God, am your playmate!
I will lead the child in you in wonderful ways
for I have chosen you.
                    —MECHTHILD OF MAGDEBURG

Recently we were told the story of Chloë, a little girl of five who loves to explore the woods near her home with her dad. Occasionally on their excursions into the woods Chloë would suddenly stop, point her little finger, and say, "Look, Dad, there's God."

The first time it happened, her dad said, "What does God look like, Chloë?" Puzzled, Chloë looked up at him and replied, "Can't you see, Dad? She's real pretty and has a long black-and-white dress on." At other times this little blond, blue-eyed girl has also described God as having dark hair and brown skin.

"How do you know it's God, Chloë?" her dad countered.

"Dad!" she replied in an exasperated tone, "everyone knows who God is."

Months passed, and though Chloë and her dad spent many days exploring the woods, the little girl never mentioned seeing God. Then one day she stopped again, pointed into the woods, and said, "Dad, see? God's here again."

"Why don't you go over and talk to her, Chloë?"

"You know why, Dad." answered Chloë.

"No, I don't."

"Because God comes to you. You don't go to her."

Is little Chloë, who has never been exposed to children's Bible school or been raised in what might be called a religious atmosphere, making God up, or is she seeing into a very real world and understanding with a wisdom far beyond her years?

One way to understand Chloë's experience is as a manifestation of the Black Madonna. This image is described through people's experience of her as a new consciousness that is manifesting itself in dreams.

> It has not yet reached the conscious level in the everyday world, but people who are in relationship to their dreams are contacting something that's quite new. It's coming through in metaphor, in images. . . . Sometimes she's crying. Sometimes she's austere. She's dark . . . because she's unknown to consciousness. . . . She is nature impregnated by spirit, accepting her own body as the chalice of the spirit. She has to do with the sacredness of matter, the intersection of sexuality and spirituality. Rejected by the patriarchy, her energy has been smoldering. It is now erupting in individuals and in the planet, demanding *conscious* recognition. Integrating what she symbolizes involves the redemption of matter. . . . The Black Madonna usually appears outdoors, so she's related to na-

ture. . . . We have to connect to her because the power that drives the patriarchy, the power that is raping the earth, the power drive behind addictions, has to be transformed. There has to be a counterbalance to all that frenzy, annihilation, ambition, competition and materialism.[1]

There is an interesting difference between Chloë's experience and the one just described. Chloë sees God, as she calls her. At five, Chloë is young enough that the inner world is still as real to her as the material world. She is still able to perceive God as an ordinary part of experience, layered into the world around us.

Babies are born with a "sixth sense"—an intuitive awareness of the unspoken thoughts and unexpressed feelings of their adult care givers. In being with children it quickly becomes apparent that adults, no matter how hard they try, can't cover up their feelings of tension and turmoil, sadness or pain. Children respond to these hidden realities by becoming anxious, irritable, solicitous, guilty, or quietly content to play alone in another room.

Children move naturally between the seen and unseen worlds of reality. When safe and unthreatened they easily unite the two—through imagination. Is the gentle lion a child plays with in the living room on a rainy afternoon

---

[1]"The Conscious Feminine," an interview with Marion Woodman by Barbara Goodrich-Dunn in *Common Boundary,* March-April 1989, pp. 10–17. A difference between the cases Woodman reports and Chloë's experience is that the woman's dress is *black-and-white,* not dark alone. Quite possibly this difference is signifying a higher level of consciousness that is beginning to rise up with greater clarity as we approach the millennium.

more or less real than the parent who gives the child a horseback ride in the same room that evening?

Could it be that babies are born into this world remembering where they came from and why they are here? Is that why they see, understand, and feel so at home in the invisible world? If so, during childhood, in learning to adapt and relate to their physical environment, they slowly lose that awareness, and the doors to the invisible world of soul gently swing shut.

For the next twenty to thirty years the task for a person growing up in the modern world is one of learning the lessons that life presents to us. Through education, relationships, training, and experience, the circumstances of life become opportunities to grow wise in the ways of the world.

After a time we are called, gently and not so gently, to reopen the doors to the world of soul that quietly closed in childhood. Through intuition and imagination, as well as through life experience, we're invited to explore the woodlands of soul, where sunshine and shadows interplay. For a moment we'll see clearly something that, in the next moment, has disappeared into the silent shadows. Did we really see it? How long will it take to restore the trust, understanding, and wisdom of the child—the Chloë—who lives within each of us?

Perhaps few have understood or appreciated the maturing creative power of positive imagination and intuition better than Albert Einstein. Once when he was asked how a person became a great theorist, Einstein replied by saying that, unless a person had been introduced to fairy tales as a child, becoming a theorist would be quite impossible. A theorist developing hypotheses must have free and open access to the realm of imagination and intuition. These were gifts that Einstein was encouraged to explore and develop in childhood through the delightful mediation of fairy tales. The process that Einstein used in science is the same process used in soul making.

As small children we were at home in the inner world of the feminine; in growing up, we have learned to be at home in the outer world of the masculine. The process of soul making isn't simply returning to what we once knew, but returning for a definite purpose. We reenter the invisible world of soul to re-member, to unite what has been divided, to heal and renew what is scarred and disfigured.

From Compulsion to Communion

As important and necessary as it is to recognize, accept, and understand the pattern of compulsion that controls our life, that is only the first step. To stop there would be like having an obsessive fascination with death, for *compulsion is the process of disintegration,* not integration and creative unity.

The final vision the Enneagram holds before us, however, is even greater than simply bringing our three centers of intelligence into balance. The vision is for a *balanced unity—harmony.* When this happens, all three centers of intelligence are creatively integrated, though each remains separate and possesses unique strengths, talents, and resources. This union impregnates a new and higher center of intelligence that holds new potential for expanding and transcending all our former limitations of understanding and consciousness.

Thus, we give birth to something new in us, a level of existence that integrates the three centers and yields the transcendent fourth, the Center of Communion. In this way, in the Enneagram Riddle (see the Introduction), *three become four*. The union, the "being one with," of which the Center of Communion speaks is a union within and without and a union that reaches to our personal depths as well as to transcendent heights.

Having taken the interior journey, we have done enough inner work that we welcome all parts and experiences of ourselves. We remember who we are, and so we can re-member who we are. No part of us is discarded, rejected, or lost; rather, through healing and transformation the good in all is revealed, and all are welcomed. Our feminine inner selves unite with our masculine outward expression, giving life to each other.

We also recognize the emergence of this center in our union with others, in our moment-by-moment recognition of other people's dignity, worth, and value. Our sense of oneness with our own human nature calls us to union with all beings who share it. In this way, the human community is re-membered.

Our journey into the depths of our own souls has grounded us in our own existence. Owning our own intuition and imagination, we are able to think for ourselves, express positive feeling, and act with integrity. We are reconnected, re-membered, with all that is of the earth, and we discover the sacredness of the mundane.

Finally and mysteriously, our journey into our depths reconnects with our heights—our human spirit and the Divine Spirit who commune and share life. Being re-membered with God creates a new vitality, because meaning, purpose, and destiny are revealed in that union.

We are re-membered by remembering, by telling and retelling our stories until we find healing as all the pieces of our lives begin to reconnect. Thus, as we increase our efforts to become soul makers, reclaiming the vision and meaning for our lives, we are also becoming soul makers of the world. Because a soul maker is one who strives to become conscious, every effort—however great or feeble—to overcome negativity, every act of kindness, every effort to grow in compassion and understanding, not only transforms the individual, but is metamorphosed into the pure light of universal consciousness. Every positive action is sacred, consecrating humanity, the world, the universe to Communion—to Love.

Ours is a work of unifying, integrating, and healing. By taking time to walk through the woodlands of the soul—through meditation, prayer, imagination, and listening—our presence invites what has been hidden in shadows to stand in the sunlight. Our presence summons Presence—Shekinah, the feminine principle of creation. Our presence makes it possible for the unconscious to become conscious, the invisible to become visible, the darkness to become light, the wound to become blessing, and the transparent Face of God within to become apparent in the world, until at last we have become one—within and without. It is the creative process, the process of unity through Love.

Soul making is the delicate hard work of learning to hold the sacred treasure of life—our own and others'—in open hands. Through many failures and some successes our soul grows until eventually we can see—with the eyes of our heart—that we have become part of a living, breathing icon called the Universe.

Centers: A New Understanding

By this time in our journey into the Enneagram and soul making, the significance of directing our attention to the three centers of intelligence has taken on a new clarity. Compulsion breeds compulsion. We waste our energy when we attempt to rearrange our compulsively patterned behavior to fit someone else's patterned behavior. Our compulsive behavior patterns—although a magnificent tribute to the will of the human spirit to survive—are not the source of our difficulty but only the symptom. The actual damage occurred in our Repressed Center.

In 1992 the entire underground system of tunnels in downtown Chicago—which is like a city unto itself—was flooded with water from the Chicago River. The city shut down. Sometime earlier, there had been official reports of severe damage to the underground retaining wall that held back the powerful waters of the river; included were recommendations for immediate repair.

But rather than follow these recommendations, officials began a long process of accepting bids, so that the repair might be done for the least possible cost. Many commentators on the disaster implied, however (and not very subtly), that there were many hidden, self-serving reasons why repairs were not accomplished post-haste. Be that as it may, the officials waited too long, and the most conservative estimates of the cost of the entire episode exceeded a billion dollars.

Similarly, when we attempt to repair our lives and our relationships for the least possible cost, we're setting ourselves up for an underground disaster. The unconscious, our underground system, will break through with a flood of outrage and self-justifying anger that will increase the very behavior we ostensibly wanted to change. At that point, our efforts will be directed at damage control, at great cost to ourselves and our relationships.

Anyone who wants to become strong and healthy spiritually, psychologically, or relationally can do so only by focusing personal effort and work on the area that has been weakened, the area of damage and stress. Thus, we must focus our energy on our Repressed Center, bringing it into balance and harmony by relieving the undue pressure that has been building up through the years.

The engineering procedures required to repair Chicago's underground tunnel wall were well understood, but there are no absolutely right or wrong ways to repair the damage to the Repressed Center, no right or wrong points at which to start the process. Although the soul making process will look different for everyone, there are some common lessons that can guide us on our journey.

To begin, we need to examine what we know of the three centers of intelligence. Our perceptions and descriptions of them are flawed. Because our understanding of them comes from the ways people overuse and therefore distort the pure beauty of each center, our understandings are based in yet another form of illusion. In this chapter, then, we will look with new eyes at the essential nature of each of the three centers. To conclude, we'll explore the treasures that our forgotten child has been guarding for us through the years.

The Intellectual Center

We identify the Intellectual Center with the head, and we commonly understand functions like thinking, calculating, deciding, and getting an objective point of view with the head. However, the Intellectual Center has a higher purpose as well. It is the kind of intelligence that produces vision. Through it, we gain a breadth and depth of awareness that leads to a profound understanding of all of life.

Natural resources.   To accomplish this task, the Intellectual Center relies on important inherent assets. First of all, it is the origin of new ideas. Mental originality and inventiveness pour forth as its firstfruits. It also is the source of possibilities. It perceives untapped potential. It penetrates the mysteries of life and imagines the unimaginable.

This center discovers keys to the doors of humanity's hopes and dreams as it journeys into the exalted world of ideals. Its understanding of human values and respect for individual diversity are the fountainhead of true objective understanding.

Another aspect of the true nature of this center is pondering. It is quietly able to reflect on situations and ideas until it penetrates complexity and reveals simple solutions. It interconnects that which is seen with spiritual realities, and thus it is the center of mystical unveiling—that spiritual intuition which reveals the Truth. Both the Bhagavad Gita and the Gospel of John proclaim in its name, "I am the Truth."

Symbols and images. Another way of understanding each center is through symbols and images that represent it. The Intellectual Center is the center of initiation and is associated with the Divine Spirit who hovered over the void, as Genesis describes it, inaugurating the process of creation. Thus, the mystery of overshadowing uniquely belongs to this center—the ability to trust in the darkness, to risk waiting in faith for the first rays of dawn, to risk waiting for the unknown other to emerge.

Nature is replete with the beauty of this center. Every breath we take reminds us of the initiation of our lives, when breath came into a body that otherwise would have been lifeless. Every seed speaks of this kind of initiation, for it contains the potential of all fulfillment. Spring—the season of seeds and new beginnings—is pregnant with possibilities reminiscent of the power this center manifests.

Flowing water—a stream or a waterfall—also speaks to us of the nature of this center. One can drink from, wash

in, and play in flowing water. You don't have to do anything to flowing water for it to be life-giving. Rather, you
receive life from it, you are refreshed simply by being in
its presence, listening to its sound or allowing its soft,
flowing nature to caress you.

But you cannot take flowing water with you; to remain flowing it cannot be corralled or possessed. Thus,
water flows through this center, not to it.

Inwardly, however, you can always experience flowing
water through the inner eye, the eye of the mind. In this
way, the Intellectual Center is the center of vision. Our
eyes transmit information and knowledge of things outside ourselves, and our inner eye sees ourselves and sees
deeply into the true nature of reality.

When it is operating true to form, then, the mastery of
the Intellectual Center is consciousness, for consciousness is the awareness that is created by the choice to acknowledge what one perceives about oneself, no matter
how painful or devastating to egocentricity. The Intellectual Center, then, is the receptive home of Divine Light—
the ability to see clearly, to see the Truth.

The Relational Center

Normally we identify the Relational Center with the
heart, and some might not see it as a function of intelligence at all. As a matter of fact, some have viewed it as
the source of irrationality and thus at odds with intelli-

gence. But this is hardly surprising, because we lack understanding of the depth and power of this center.

The true purpose of the Relational Center clearly reveals it as an authentic kind of intelligence. Connectedness, relatedness, and transcendence are the result when this center is used properly. In other words, the purpose of this center is to propel us outside ourselves, to connect us with realities foreign to our own limited experience. This truly is a kind of intelligence of which humanity is in great need, for it creates wholesome and healthy relationship with self, others, the universe, and God.

Natural resources.   To accomplish this formidable task, the Relational Center draws upon its native strengths. Incarnation is first among them—the ability to make the intangible tangible, to make the invisible world visible through word and feeling.

This is also the center that synthesizes; it combines diverse realities, reorganizing them into a coherent whole that transcends previously accepted limitations. It integrates random and seemingly unrelated perceptions, translating them into understandable terms that give direction and meaning to life.

This center is also able to hear the cry for freedom and dignity in every human heart. It is at its best when it perceives the deeper realities in people. By applying philosophical and spiritual truth to daily life and by yearning for all that is Good, it finds its practical bent. Thus, both the Bhagavad Gita and the Gospel of John proclaim in its name, "I am the Way."

Symbols and images.   The Relational Center is the center of manifestation, of epiphany; thus, it is associated with the divine as Healer—in Christianity with the Christ, and in Buddhism with Krishna. Its formative mystery is redemption through the shaman, the one who unites heaven and earth. It is also the center of the artist, who gives shape and form to feelings and ideas.

In nature this center is revealed in planting and growing, which gives expression to the potential of the seed. The union of sun, rain, soil, and seed produces fruit, food, and beauty. Summer is the season that expresses this center.

Fire is another expression of spiritual energy and mysticism, and therefore it is regarded as a unifying and stabilizing element. It is a symbol of transformation and regeneration. However, because fire can either purify or destroy, its nature must be respected. Thus, this center carries the flame but cannot contain the flame.

The uses of fire speak further of this center. Meals are prepared over a fire; from time immemorial sharing a meal has been a symbol of the sharing of hearts. People also warm themselves around a fire, and as they relax and rest they become reflective and intimate with one another. Fire is associated with life and health, passion and love.

This is the center of union, whose symbol is the ear. Through our ears we receive personal knowledge of other people, and our inner ear perceives the longings of the human soul.

The mastery of this center is process—understanding human growth, development, healing, and renewal. It is the receptive home of Divine Love; through it we transcend ourselves.

The Creative Center

Through the Creative Center of intelligence we complete the work of being a person in the world. If set free, the true nature of this intelligence would cause a radical conversion to joy. The joy and power of creating would necessarily overcome victimization, for violence cannot exist where there is respect for the dignity of human life.

Natural resources.   Because it is the center of freedom, the Creative Center is the home of play and fun. Playfulness yields healing and balance and awakens us to possibilities. Through it, we communicate our true nature and express ourselves simply for the world to see.

This center also accomplishes goals, because it has an innate sense of timing regarding how to proceed, how to make things happen. It is able to approach a situation, taking it stage by stage and dealing with each new advancement to create progress. The Creative Center finds peace and happiness in work.

This intelligence knows how to bring a project to completion, how to realize a goal, how to actualize concepts. Through it, we have access to the material world. This center's ease with material reality releases knowledge of how to effect change by using proven and reliable resources.

Then it rearranges and transposes these elements in an endless series of original creations.

It is the center that effects the prophetic word and leads the way toward unity. It is a storehouse of innovation—that kind of creativity that arises from direct perception of practical matters. This center knows how to produce the Beautiful. In its name both the Bhagavad Gita and the Gospel of John proclaim, "I am the Life."

Symbols and images. The Creative Center embraces and delights in all of life; thus, it is associated with the Father/Mother God, the Divine Creator. Its mystery is nurturing. Through it, we discover the pleasure of sublimating our egocentric desires for higher principles—for the well-being of another or for the collective good. Its inner sense of guidance and outer focus on accomplishment recognize and call forth gifts and talents.

Yielding foundation, boldness, and steadfastness, this center produces that inner discipline we need to follow a chosen direction. Its gift is presence—the ability to stand firm in a situation, to be with others in meaningful ways, to take responsibility.

Its season of the year is autumn, the time of abundant fulfillment, the time of celebration, festivals, and gratitude. The Creative Center exults in the sensual, erotic pleasure of being alive. The earth is an apt symbol of this Center, for the earth receives all that she is given, and even in death nothing is lost but rather transformed into new life.

However, to continue its yield and maintain its richness, the earth must be respected rather than abused.

Thus, this center belongs to the earth, but the earth does not belong to it.

When the essential nature of the Creative Center is functioning properly, we know how to live in appropriate relationship with the earth, using its resources to sustain life without abusing them. This center guides us in using the things of the earth to create artifacts of practical and artistic beauty. Out of this center, as out of the darkness and depth of the earth, flows the wisdom of death and the wonder of birth.

The Creative Center is the center of actualization, whose symbol is the mouth. Through our mouths we state our goals, principles, and ideals. Verbalization is the expression of commitment and dedication to effect change. Through our inner talk we motivate ourselves for expenditure of energy. Other bodily symbols are hands and feet, through which we focus our energy on empowering ourselves and others—making ideals real in the world.

The mastery of this center is creativity—bringing an idea to expression in the outer world. It is the receptive home of Divine Life, and through it we experience the ongoing, mysterious union of the human and the divine.

The Child: Divine Mystic and Creator of Unity

A child like Chloë lives in each of us, a child who sees into the mystical realm of the divine and understands the spiritual nature of the universe. This level of reality is veiled to our adult eyes that have been clouded by the attitude we call realism, which is often cynicism in disguise. It is often that very cynicism that makes the child's world seem unreal, when indeed it offers a needed balance and a universal perspective. Recovery of this inner child and healing of the inner child are themes that have been popular in certain spiritual and therapeutic approaches. To those not involved in these disciplines, however, the importance they place on recovering the inner child is mystifying.

The Enneagram offers a way to understand this dimension of life and integrate it into the wider perspective: the maturing of the individual and the healing of society. In order to achieve this perspective, however, we need to go back and gather several threads of thought presented earlier in this book.

The dream that precipitated our journey into the soul-making dimensions of the Enneagram (recorded in the Introduction of this book) leapt beyond the known boundaries of understanding about this extraordinary wisdom. Our appreciation for this ancient knowledge quickly grew into an almost reverential awe as we realized that the interpreter in the dream was revealing a new and deeper dimension of the dignity and beauty hidden beneath the layers of illusion described by the Enneagram.

The three centers of intelligence were described in a new way. All previous descriptions portrayed the centers as they appear when overused. It's difficult to describe the excitement and gratitude we felt as we recognized that for some inexplicable reason we were being allowed to catch a glimpse of the pure, essential nature of each center. The awesome reality of the three centers of intelligence is the core of the Enneagram and reveals how it is much more than a personality typing tool. Understanding this, the true meaning of the Enneagram began to unfold as gently as the petals of a spring flower.

Another dimension of the dream, one that relates to the equality of the three centers of intelligence, is revealed as the interpretation begins and a faceless voice says, "Now I will interpret your dream for you," and then after a long pause, "Now I will interpret the Creed for you." At this point in the dream it was absolutely clear that the creed to which the voice referred was the Nicene Creed, which is why Kathy thought the interpreter's statement was so strange. What did this dream have to do with the statement of faith based upon the doctrinal decisions made by bishops of the Catholic church at the first Council of Nicea in 325 C.E.?[2]

As stated in chapter 1, when we first referred to several of the general councils of the Catholic church, this research is based on these councils not because we are writing for a Christian audience only, but because whether we

---

[2]The text of the Nicene Creed reads: "We believe in one God, the Father, the Almighty, maker of heaven and earth, of all that is seen and unseen.

"We believe in one Lord, Jesus Christ, the only Son of God, eternally begotten of the Father, God from God, Light from Light, true God from true God, begotten, not made, one in being with the Father. Through him all things were made. For us men and for our salvation he came down from heaven: by the power of the Holy Spirit he was born of the Virgin Mary, and became man. For our sake he was crucified under Pontius Pilate; he suffered, died, and was buried. On the third day he

are Christian or not, we live in a culture that has been shaped by the Christian experience. Christianity has played the leading role in and therefore defined soul development for Western culture; in its doctrines and history are hidden the secrets of this culture's healing or the seeds of its demise.

———— ————

rose again in fulfillment of the Scriptures; he ascended into heaven and is seated at the right hand of the Father. He will come again in glory to judge the living and the dead, and his kingdom will have no end.

"We believe in the Holy Spirit, the Lord, the giver of life, who proceeds from the Father [and the Son]. With the Father and the Son he is worshipped and glorified. He has spoken through the Prophets.

"We believe [in] one, holy, catholic, and apostolic church. We acknowledge one baptism for the forgiveness of sins. We look for the resurrection of the dead, and the life of the world to come. Amen."

The phrase *and the Son* in the third paragraph is bracketed because it was not in the original Greek text but was added by local custom in the kingdom of Charlemagne sometime during the eighth century. It became a part of the creed in the West but never in the East; indeed, it was a subject of hot controversy between the Western (Roman) and Eastern (Greek) churches until they split from each other in the Great Schism of 1054 C.E., with this phrase being the centerpiece of their differences. That schism created the Orthodox churches as distinct entities from the Roman Catholic Church.

This dispute seems like a dreadfully unimportant technicality to cause such a profound rift in Christianity until its meaning is understood. The Orthodox position is that if the Son is begotten of the Father but the Spirit proceeds from the Father *and* the Son, then the Spirit is subordinate to the Son. Since the Spirit is "the giver of life," the Orthodox Church said that the work of grace, in their term the "deification of humanity," would be lessened and even cease if the Spirit's authority was weakened in this way. Since giving life is the true purpose of spirituality, the issue is of paramount importance.

The word *in* in the last paragraph is bracketed because it does not appear in the original Greek text or in the official Latin translations from the Greek, but it is commonly inserted in contemporary English translations of this text. When you consider it carefully, the difference between believing someone and believing *in* someone is enormous, but in daily speech the two are often interchanged.

Our interest lies precisely in the connection the dream made between the three centers of intelligence and the three persons of God described in the creed; the Spirit is associated with the Intellectual Center, the Healer (the Son) with the Relational Center, and the Father/Mother (the Father) with the Creative Center.

If you read the text of the creed (in note 1 of this chapter), you will find it describes a God who is three persons united in one nature, God the Father, the Son, and the Spirit. Eight of the creedal statements concern God the Father, twenty-three statements refer to the Son, and five statements are about the Spirit. This unequal treatment of the three equal persons of the Christian Divine Trinity is easily explained from a historical perspective.

The first three hundred years of reflection on Christian experience brought to the surface many different and conflicting ideas of who Jesus of Nazareth was and how he related to all the persons of the Trinity. Consequently, when the bishops of the church gathered for their first general council, their preoccupation was to settle these disputes and to proclaim clearly what they believed was authentic Christian teaching about Jesus, in whom they saw the manifestation of the Son. Since the Father and the Spirit were less the subjects of controversy, the bishops paid less attention to stating beliefs about them.

The Christian churches have considered the Nicene Creed to be a summary of belief about the nature of God since it was written in the fourth century. Whenever people wanted a concise explanation of a Christian understanding of the Deity, they consulted this statement of faith.

Statements about God are at the core of individuals' and cultures' belief systems and therefore of their worldview as well. A careful examination of Christianity's and therefore Western culture's worldview reveals that inequality and imbalance are built into it. In saying that it would interpret the Creed, Kathy's dream proposes an equality and a balance within human beings that will manifest itself in the society that they create. It suggests that a profound and powerful shift in our thinking and in our worldview is at the core of the healing our society seeks, the promotion of honesty, sincerity, and truth.

Until this shift takes place within us, we will retain our ability to survive, but the vision of wholeness revealed in Kathy's dream will never be realized: the *"triune bonding that will yield the fourth and final companion (center) needed to release the human spirit to transcend the limitations of the human."* For the triune bonding to become experiential, we must unite with our Repressed Center; in doing so, we treat all the centers equally and thus are interiorly balanced.

However, balance is not a static state. As these three kinds of intelligence experience themselves as healthy, a new potential is awakened, the potential of a new dimension of intelligence—the Center of Communion. In the dream, human beings were described as a "children" created, protected, and nurtured by the Spirit, the Healer, or the Father/Mother God. We have been created, protected, and nurtured by the God image associated with our *Dominant Center*—the center of survival that has created our personality, protected, and nurtured us in life up to the present moment. Yet, if we choose to remain focused in this center, the dream says, our life journey will become a tormented survival.

Thus, we must awaken and bond with the child of our forgotten center—for this is God's child—the Divine Child. The balance and equality among the centers this bonding creates allows the fourth center, the mystic center of spirituality, to emerge. In this way another line of the Enneagram Riddle (see the Introduction) is resolved: *Then three become four.*

The wounded child within—the Divine Child, our hidden self—is found in our Repressed Center. Brought to consciousness, it makes a new home in the source of our spiritual power and creativity, the Center of Communion. Through the child within, we will be empowered to move from multiplicity to unity. By touching the Center of Communion we will be taught and come to understand the meaning of our life, for this is where our destiny, our heart's desire, will be revealed to us.

The Center of Communion also relates to a final element of the modern research on the brain, which we touched upon in chapter 2. There we applied this research to the ancient understanding of three centers of intelligence. Let's review and summarize this data: The human brain is now known to have three layers, each of which relate to one of the three centers—the ancient reptilian or physical brain has the same functions at the Creative Center; the mammalian brian, the emotional-relational brain, is the home of the Relational Center; and the neocortex or rational brain is associated with the Intellectual Center.

Scientists say of the three brains exactly what the Enneagram says of the three centers, that they must be integrated for a person to be healthy. When the three brains are integrated, for example, they pass information to each other, each adding its own perspective so that a person's response will be in his or her own and society's best interests. Some modern commentators link the growing social ills of our culture to the way we promote the nonintegration of the three brains. When the three brains are not integrated, these commentators say, people think one thing, feel another, and do a third. Neurosis is the result of this lack of interior unity, and social ills must result outwardly because people's actions are not informed and moderated by careful thought and personal and emotional considerations.[3] This is clearly a similar if not the same message that the Enneagram teaches: the necessity of uniting the three centers in equal balance.

But there is a final element of scientific research that now also finds a context within the teaching of the Enneagram. It has to do with the neocortex, the thinking, rational brain. An element of modern brain research that has become part of our common cultural knowledge is that we only use 10 percent of our brains. This idea is not really quite accurate, however, because it is the *neocortex* that remains mostly unused; we develop and use our physical and emotional brains 100 percent, but together they comprise one-fifth of our brains by weight. We only use 10 or 20 percent of our neocortex; 80 percent of our

---

[3]For example, cf. "The Roots of Intelligence," by Dr. Joseph Chilton Pearce (Boulder, CO: Sounds True Recordings, 1989).

neocortex is not used because it is not needed for even a highly sensitive, genius brain to function properly.

What is this unused neocortex for? In all of creation, scientists have not found a smidgeon of reality that has no purpose. What could the purpose of the unused portion of our brains be?

The Enneagram teaches that we are meant to integrate all three centers, not two centers and part of a third. Simultaneously, the Enneagram teaches the absolute necessity of waking up (consciousness) and of conversion (openness to the new idea that I and what concerns me are not the center of the universe) for a person to come to wholeness. Personal effort supported by grace is the formula the Enneagram offers for the well-being of individuals and of society.

Aware of this, it was especially gratifying to learn of the opinions of Dr. Joseph Chilton Pearce who has raised similar questions about integration of the three brains, about the effects of nonintegration within the brain upon personal and social development, and about the purpose of the 80 percent of the neocortex of which the brain has no need for the normal purposes of thinking.[4]

Could it be that this part of the brain opens in the spiritual quest, that it is the home of the Center of Communion, the fourth and final companion by which we will transcend the limits of our human experience as we now know it? Surely, humanity awaits this kind of mystic, transcendent breakthrough. If the religions of the

---

[4]Cf. "The Roots of Intelligence."

world have given us only part of the spiritual answer or, as some have experienced, even misled people in the spiritual path, that sad reality need not make us mistrust the spiritual journey. Instead, it can create a more open stance to all of life, a stance that will allow us the freedom to question, to trust in our own inner wisdom, to be courageous enough to challenge ourselves to search for truth, and to be risk takers who dare to love. For the spiritual journey is an inward and personal quest that will, if it is genuine, lead us into a communal expression.

The child is the symbol of this mystic center within us—the center of reawakening and transformation, the Center of Communion. In this context, the Divine Child must be understood as wisdom and creativity. We must clearly identify oversimplified and romanticized notions of childhood and being childlike so that they can be transcended. Thus, we are not speaking here of the child as a return to pseudoinnocence, or to a nonpolitical, immature stance toward the world. Rather, like Jung, we choose to experience the Divine Child in the fullness of its transformative power.

The mystic child is symbolically known as the one who solves riddles and signals the time has come for great spiritual change. Psychologically speaking, the child is of the soul and is the unifying symbol of the unconscious and conscious. Jung said, "The child paves the way for future change of personality."

Free, uncomplicated, spontaneous, and filled with life and vitality, the child—close to the earth and united with the eternal God who lives within—is the symbol of the future.

Through the eyes of our child we will, like Chloë, be able to perceive the God who dwells in the woodlands of the earth. When we see Her we will remember our destiny and, like Chloë, understand that "God comes to you."

For Personal and Group Work

1. The work of Marion Woodman and others speaks of the emergence of a feminine expression of God in images like the Black Madonna and Shekinah emerging from the collective unconscious of humanity through dreams. Frequently when God is referred to or described in feminine terms or images, people instantly have intense reactions—everything from anger and fear to unbridled enthusiasm and affirmation.

How do you respond to these images? What is your response to the idea that a feminine expression of God is emerging in the world today? If this idea gives you life, describe the freedom you feel. If these ideas seem extreme and outlandish, describe your feelings and thoughts as well. Can you relate your responses to any beliefs you were taught and have not questioned, or to any experiences of disillusionment by authorities you unquestioningly believed in? What gifts in your Repressed Center could help to moderate your responses?

2. The first fascination of the Enneagram is with its accurate descriptions of the nine personality compulsions. Has this perspective been true for you? How do you respond to the statement that to focus on the compulsive dimension of each pattern "would be like having an obsessive fascination with death, for compulsion is the process of disintegration, not of creative unity"?

3. Compulsion breeds compulsion. Can you identify times when you felt good—on top of the world—and someone came at you with negative comments or attitudes? How long were you able to maintain your upbeat approach? How does remembering this incident help you understand the power of negative emotions?

4. This chapter presents a new vision of the three centers of intelligence, naming clearly the gifts they are meant to bring to a life that uses them in balance. In what general areas of life do you find your greatest struggles: discovering a personal vision for your life (the gift of the Intellectual Center), developing personal relationships and expressing your emotions and vision in a life-giving way (the gift of the Relational Center), or actualizing your ideas and plans in the world (the gift of the Creative Center)? How does the lack of the gifts that lie in your Repressed Center prevent you from living a full life?

5. This chapter presents a vision of unity possible within every person, explaining that when the three centers of intelligence live in balance and harmony they yield a fourth center, the Center of Communion. How would you begin to imagine and describe the meaning of this fourth center in your life?

7

Profiles of God

———

Being received by a God
other than ourselves
makes it possible for us
to receive this hidden
God into us.
—ANN BELFORD ULANOV

We have been traveling together on a journey inward, a trip that has led us to the depths of our own inner selves. This journey has been as real as any pilgrimage one could take to a shrine or holy place in the world.

A pilgrimage is a special time set aside in which people forgo their ordinary schedules and responsibilities, often putting up with not a few inconveniences, for the sake of touching something extraordinary, something sacred. The meaning, the reason, for pilgrimages is that there is a deep need in all of us to touch something or someone greater than ourselves. We long to know and be known, to touch and be touched by the holy, the good, the true, the beautiful—by Love.

There is a longing within us to experience for ourselves the wonder of meaning, goodness, truth, beauty, and love. Yet we find ourselves caught in the demands of everyday living, and if we allow these to take all our time—and we all know that they can eat up every waking minute and then some—we'll never know who we can really be. We'll never touch our greatness.

We live in a world of information in which we have to "keep up" with one or more topics like technological or professional developments, family interests, community affairs, personal finances, and so on. Where is the time for delving into the truth of eternal realities, spiritual truth?

Sensing our own deep spiritual hunger, we feel empty, and we may dream about having a month to get away from daily life to pursue spirituality, or about finding a quiet place to which we could retreat and develop our spiritual life. Again, we feel trapped in the harsh, either-or world of dualism. Our minds crave the satisfying pleasure that comes with a wide breadth of knowledge, and our hearts ache to be drawn into the depths of spiritual truth, wisdom, and mystery.

Further, we long to believe but fear playing the fool. It's good to know about spirituality, but is it really healthy to get caught up in it? So we try to understand spiritual truth with our objective minds. However, approaching it in this way prevents us from taking truth into our being in a way that is vulnerable, personal, and, yes, truly human.

Although there is a great spiritual hunger being expressed in our society today, we also face a great obstacle: we've become secular cynics and religious agnostics. Too afraid to risk belief in that which we can't prove inductively, we remain empty within. We have forgotten how to pay attention to or recognize the holy, the sacred, either within ourselves or in the world. It seems that we are struggling with the problem of belief or faith. Maurice Nicoll, a British psychologist and teacher of the wisdom undergirding the Enneagram, equated the virtue of faith with vision. Has the modern world lost its vision, its faith in God?

The Problem of Belief

In our culture what do we make of "God talk"? The German philosopher Friedrich Nietzsche described the problem a century ago when he proclaimed, "God is dead." In making this statement he was not rejoicing, he was lamenting. Claiming to be verbalizing what he saw and felt around him, he declared that Western culture had lost the ability to affirm any basis for knowledge or truth.

In the decades since, we have seen the accuracy of his proclamation. At various points and in different ways, our culture has generally rejected the customary beliefs in morality, religion, ethics, and government. Jung also noticed this phenomenon occurring in the interior world, observing that the Christian God-image, that which expresses the meaning of life in the West, was fading from his patients' dreams. He also mused on the despair and aggression in modern Western art, intuiting in these creations an anguished cry over the death of God who gives life meaning.[1]

But if the question is one of belief, there is a more important emptiness of belief we must examine. In generation after generation this culture has not communicated to people the ability to believe in themselves. This is the true sorrow—ought we say madness?—in the way we think, feel, and believe. Our insistence on rationalistic values has left us devoid of imagination and intuition—those very qualities we need to build the Great Bridge of soul and find our footing in the exalted world of spirit. Without the tools we need to explore our inner terrain—sometimes without even an ability to *see* the terrain or believe it's real—we have been forced to live with an entirely materialistic worldview that validates us neither in our bodies nor in our souls and spirits.

In other civilizations belief in a transcendent reality and in being part of both a material and a spiritual world has been commonplace, an integral component of daily life. These traditional beliefs and values were stable, and though they seem unsophisticated by modern standards, they nonetheless provided a quality in life that helped people to accept and overcome life's difficulties. This quality is *meaning*.

Religion claims to perceive an unseen level of reality that can be understood in depth only through symbol.

---

[1]C. G. Jung and Marie-Louise von Franz, Joseph L. Henderson, Jolande Jacobi, Aniela Jaffé, *Man and His Symbols* (New York: Dell, 1964), pp. 295, 314.

However, the rationalistic thought and materialistic assumptions of modern Western culture have all but destroyed people's ability to think and perceive symbolically. Instead, symbols are taken literally. They are made so concrete that the multidimensional layers of meaning in them are lost even to many people who want to understand them, let alone to the unreflective person. Consequently, the symbols that were meant to be windows to a spiritual world are treated as gods demanding superstitious belief and rigid loyalty.

The knowledge and sophistication of the modern world has not eliminated the human need for meaning, however. It has created a void of meaning, because people can no longer accept immature, simplistic, rigid, or superstitious beliefs, and religion often hasn't reformulated the belief system it offers in a way that would be more open and welcoming to the questioning, thoughtful seeker.

Many of the mainline religions remain blind and deaf to what people are saying: that they can no longer accept a belief system that imposes guilt and promotes prejudice instead of nurturing life. Patriarchal leaders respond by feeling they must close ranks to regain and exercise more control. Is it any wonder, then, that people go from church to church, group to group, teacher to teacher in search of truth and meaning for their lives?

Without the inner certainty that the individual person is loved, important, and part of a greater and larger world than the one visible to the naked eye, the ability to develop a healthy sense of self-worth or to sustain a vision of the reality of the spiritual world becomes extremely difficult. Thus, humanity searches and questions, longing for something worth believing in.

A scene from *Mass: A Theater Piece for Singers, Players and Dancers* by Leonard Bernstein expresses simply and poignantly the heart-wrenching pain in our culture on the point of belief. After the chorus sings the Mass's Credo in a rhythmic, almost militaristic monotone, a soloist sings with an intensity and anxiety that crescendos, until the chorus sings the final verse quietly and plaintively.

> *I believe in God,*
> *But does God believe in me?*
> *I'll believe in any god*
> *If any god there be . . .*
>
> *I believe in God,*
> *But then I believe in three.*
> *I'll believe in twenty gods*
> *If they'll believe in me . . .*
>
> *Who created my life?*
> *Made it come to be?*
> *Who accepts this awful*
> *Responsibility?*
>
> *Is there someone out there?*
> *If there is, then who?*
> *Are you listening to this song*
> *I'm singing just for you?*
>
> *I believe in singing.*
> *Do you believe it too?*
> *I believe each note I sing*
> *But is it getting through?*

I believe in F-sharp.
I believe in G.
But does it mean a thing to you
Or should I change my key?

How do you like A-flat?
Do you believe in C?— . . .
Do you believe in anything
That has to do with me?

I believe in God,
But does God believe in me?
I'll believe in thirty gods
If they'll believe in me . . .

I'll believe in sugar and spice,
I'll believe in everything nice;
I'll believe in you and you and you
And who . . .

Who'll believe in me?[2]

The question of belief in our culture has become a reciprocal one. It is not only a question of who believes in
God but whether God believes in us.

In the solitude of our own hearts, do not even the
most powerful, accomplished, and celebrated among us
ache for a sense of security in the universe, a sense that
we belong, that our lives have meaning, and that we are
loved by a mysterious Other? Do we not long for a
ground for our being?

---

[2]Text by Stephen Schwartz and Leonard Bernstein.

Can we believe in ourselves—not in the sense of making ourselves successful or pulling our lives together, but in the sense of believing that we ourselves are sacred, and therefore our lives have meaning, purpose, and value? Can we believe in ourselves and trust in life enough to commit radically to the values and choices that can make a difference in the world? Do we dare risk being loved? Do we dare risk loving? Can we become soul makers?

The Divine Dilemma

What if we were to find out today that there was indeed a God who loved us more than we could ever love ourselves? What if that God had more faith in us than we could ever have in ourselves? To have someone *believe* in *me!* What a joy! What a wonder! What a burden of responsibility!

Is that the problem? It seems that the modern world has perpetrated values so materialistic, so external and shallow that we are out of touch with the dignity of human life, with being created in the image of God. We can no longer bear the burden of believing in an immanent God, in a God who lives within, who is layered into our daily lives, who participates in the human adventure.

Instead, we say that the only God is a transcendent God, a God-out-there, who has little to do with human life or with me personally. Then we choose whether or not to believe in that God. It is all so safe—this God can't touch me personally anyway.

Ultimately, it makes little difference whether we believe this God doesn't exist or believe this God lives in grandeur and opulence and rules with severe justice, power, and victory, for believing in this God requires no risk on our part. If God doesn't exist, no more need be said. If God does exist, how could we, imperfect as we are, do anything more than attempt to appease this unknowable God through external religious practices? We could be safe only by following the rules. Meister Eckhart once addressed people who carried this attitude toward God:

> There are people who in penitential exercises and external practices of which they make a great deal, cling to their selfish I. May God have pity on these people who know so little of divine truth! These people are called holy because of their external appearances; but on the inside they are asses, for they do not understand at all the correct meaning of divine truth.[3]

On the other hand, what if God were to live within and walk with us on our pilgrim journey through life? What if God were most at home among the poor and weak, among the deformed and wounded? What if God's judgment were forgiveness and the only rule or law of God love and compassion? What a divine dilemma that would be!

---

[3]Quoted in "Meister Eckhart's Spiritual Journey" by Matthew Fox, in *Western Spirituality: Historical Roots, Ecumenical Routes* (Santa Fe, NM: Bear & Company, 1981), p. 231.

This is the God of love, mystery, and unity. This God lives within and walks with us on our journey into the land of soul.

Wound as womb.   This God has been with us since the moment we were created, grounding us in ourselves and connecting us with the universe. In the language of the Enneagram, this God created us in Divine Image and Likeness. Each of the three centers of intelligence reflects in human form one of the Divine Persons traditionally spoken of in Christianity: the Intellectual Center reflects the Spirit of God and the mystery of overshadowing or conceiving; the Relational Center reflects God as Healer and the mystery of incarnation; the Creative Center reflects the Father/Mother God and the mystery of creation.

Thus were we born into this world, created by God and a place in which God dwells. Soon, however, we were wounded—wounded by the egocentricity that has marred this world from the beginning. Recalling what we learned in chapter 5, we were, in the language of the Enneagram, wounded in and through one of the three centers of intelligence. Because of the wound in that center, we have associated it with pain and for this reason repress it, unable to see its value or purpose.

But the God who lives within—because this God is at home among the poor and weak, among the deformed and wounded, and because this God is a true lover and therefore loves that which needs strengthening and nourishment—has made a home in our wound, in our Repressed Center. In the moment of our Original Wound a profile of God appeared in its core. Ever since, this God has been weaving our pain into a sacred membrane, a womb where our forgotten child has been secretly cared for. Will this sacred womb become the source of new life and spiritual empowerment by giving birth to the Divine Child who dwells within? Or will it become the forgotten tomb of our unknown child? The choice is ours.

A God who believes in us.   The God who lives in that which we repress, deny, disown, and devalue is a God who does not demand that we believe but a God who believes in us. Unconcerned about asserting power over us or demanding that specific beliefs are verbalized in specific words, this God lives in the shanty town of our Repressed Center, dressed in rags, waiting to welcome us whenever we stop for a visit, no matter how brief.

Her love is the hub of life in that center of intelligence, until with conscious energy we ourselves choose to love that center and develop its native strengths appropriately. Her power is a power *under*—a strength that supports, nourishes, and makes growth possible. Can anyone be more powerful than one who delights in giving power away freely?

Profiles of God

At every moment in our life that we were open to grace, a profile or contour of the Divine Image carried within was layered into our personality. With every unselfish act or word of kindness, with every unself-conscious smile, with every loving thought, another subtle line of the profile of our Divine Image was drawn. When we consciously choose to do the work of creatively releasing the treasures hidden in our Repressed Center, we reflect more and more clearly the profile of the God who lives within.

The name of the Divine Image for each of the nine patterns of the Enneagram, like the Enneagram itself, comes from antiquity. The Jewish mystical wisdom of the Kabbalah teaches the Sefirot, the ten faces of God. The first is Crown (Keter) and is eternal; it is the nothingness or no-thingness of God. Consequently, the next in the list is considered the first, and after it follow the faces of God in Enneagramic order. Each one we find associated with the Repressed Center for that pattern.

> Achievers' (1) Divine Image is Wisdom (*Hokhmah*). As they pursue their Lifelong Quest for transformation, Achievers are crowned with the new name of Pathfinder.

> Helpers' (2) Divine Image is Understanding (*Binah*). As they pursue their Lifelong Quest for transformation, Helpers are crowned with the new name of Partner.

> Succeeders' (3) Divine Image is Love (*Hesed*). As they pursue their Lifelong Quest for transformation, Succeeders are crowned with the new name of Motivator.

> Individualists' (4) Divine Image is Power (*Gevurah*). As they pursue their Lifelong Quest for transformation, Individualists are crowned with the new name of Builder.

Observers' (5) Divine Image is Beauty (*Tif'eret*). As they pursue their Lifelong Quest for transformation, Observers are crowned with the new name of Explorer.

Guardians' (6) Divine Image is Endurance (*Nezah*). As they pursue their Lifelong Quest for transformation, Guardians are crowned with the new name of Stabilizer.

Dreamers' (7) Divine Image is Majesty (*Hod*). As they pursue their Lifelong Quest for transformation, Dreamers are crowned with the new name of Illuminator.

Confronters' (8) Divine Image is Foundation (*Yesod*). As they pursue their Lifelong Quest for transformation, Confronters are crowned with the new name of Philanthropist.

Preservationists' (9) Divine Image is Presence (*Shekhinah*). As they pursue their Lifelong Quest for transformation, Preservationists are crowned with the new name of Universalist.[4]

The diagram "Divine Image and Lifelong Quest" portrays the nine patterns of the Enneagram with the names of each as we have come to know them, the transforming

---

[4]We first wrote of Divine Image and Lifelong Quest, as well as the Kabbalah's Sefirot, in chapter 8 of *What's My Type?*

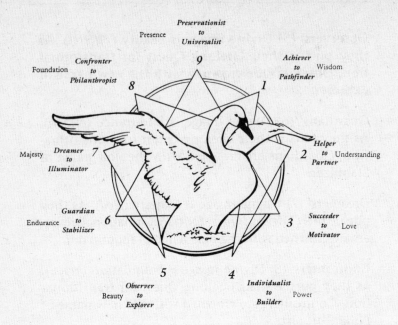

Preservationist
to
Universalist

Presence

9

Achiever
to   Wisdom
Pathfinder

Confronter
Foundation   *to*
Philanthropist

8   **1**

Dreamer   **7**
Majesty   *to*
Illuminator

Helper
to   Understanding
Partner

2

Guardian
Endurance   *to*   **6**
Stabilizer

Succeeder
to   Love
Motivator

3

5   **4**

Observer
Beauty   *to*
Explorer

Individualist
to   Power
Builder

Divine Image, and a new name for each pattern.[5] The new name is conferred on the journey into the land of soul. The conferring of a new name, like a sacred rite of passage, takes place somewhere on the person's Lifelong Quest and happens when the time is right. Do we know when we're given a new name? Of course! Does anyone else? Does it matter?

---

[5]The Enneagram is usually depicted as a circle containing a nine-point star. Our rendition has been especially designed and alters the typical presentation of the Enneagram. Most significantly, a swan occupies the center of the diagram because we use the Hans Christian Andersen's fairy tale *The Ugly Duckling* as a paradigm for the process of transformation in our book *What's My Type?*

Repressed Relational Center

Threes, Sevens, and Eights repress the Relational Center. Profiles of the Divine Image of the Healer have been layered into the contours of their lives every time they risked becoming vulnerable even for a moment. In this center of incarnation, the Divine Healer cares for the child who was wounded years ago by the pain of alienation, of separation from love. Afraid to risk becoming vulnerable again, Threes, Sevens, and Eights have held their gentle and spiritual Divine Child prisoner in the Repressed Relational Center.

Three: The Succeeder.   Love (*Hesed*), the Divine Image for Succeeders, is the core of the Relational Center. It is the indefinable word people use when they talk about the meaning and purpose of relationship. Love is that quality by which human beings transcend themselves, connecting themselves with persons and realities outside of self. It is the movement of the heart for the well-being of self as well as another, indeed, of all creation.

Like a princess held captive in the castle tower, Love lives in the secret recesses of Succeeders' Repressed Center, sentenced to a life of isolation and loneliness. Only when heroic honesty and integrity scale the tower walls do silhouettes of their Divine Image of Love become visible in their personality. Set free, Real Beautiful Self awakens and reveals the truth that openness and vulnerability will shed light on the lie that they are unlovable. This

truth opens the door to intimate relationships for Succeeders.

By allowing the love others feel for them to touch
their hearts, Succeeders learn to live in communion, thus
letting go of the need to deceive themselves and others
with image, accomplishments, and their desire for admiration. Engaging themselves in the process of human
growth, Succeeders promote others' growth and become
Motivators, bringing the community to life in myriad
ways. Artistic creation will become their forte, if not always through direct involvement in the arts themselves,
definitely in the way they shape their lives.

Seven: The Dreamer.   The Divine Image for Dreamers is
Majesty; the Hebrew word is *Hod,* sometimes translated
as Splendor or as the Beauty of the Creator. The person
who is majestic is noble, stately, dignified—qualities that
one associates with people who know themselves thoroughly and are comfortable with themselves. Such personal knowledge arises from the Relational Center, the
home of union, human growth, development, healing,
and renewal.

Thus Majesty, clothed in rags and performing menial
chores, lives hidden in the lives of Dreamers until they
discover Real Beautiful Self by facing their fear of love
and becoming vulnerable and open to the pain and joy
of relationships. With the welfare of others at the heart of
their approach to life, profiles of their Divine Image of
Majesty rise up from the earth of their souls, and their

minds emerge in all the altruistic, radiant splendor of love.

Rooted in an acceptance of self that can only come forth with great personal effort and fortitude, Dreamers surrender the protection created by their penchant for intellectualizing, preferring instead to connect with people emotionally. Sharing their hearts as well as the fruits of their mental creativity, they are given the new name *Illuminators*.

Eight: The Confronter.   Confronters' Divine Image is Foundation (*Yesod*), the cosmic pillar that upholds the world and connects heaven to earth. Its home is the Relational Center, the intelligence of connectedness and of manifestation. The Relational Center makes the world of ideals real, makes the invisible world visible through word and emotion, and relates all aspects of the world to each other—people, creation, and God.

Profiles of their Divine Image of Foundation live disguised in Confronters' armor of the warrior's aggressiveness and strength. Silhouettes of the divine are engraved into their personalities, and their true nature can be revealed with the rescuing of Real Beautiful Self. In union with their best selves, Confronters no longer need to hide their lack of inner awareness in tactics of intimidation and maneuvering for power.

Instead, they learn to love themselves, especially by compassionately giving themselves the gift of time and space to grow personally, to find healing, and to enjoy intimate relationship with others. With these qualities they find ways to use their strength to become *Philanthropists,* promoting human growth and uniting heaven's values with earth's reality.

Repressed Intellectual Center

Sixes, Ones, and Twos repress the Intellectual Center. Profiles of the Divine Image of the Spirit have been layered into the contours of their lives every time they risked believing in an eternal vision or destiny for their own lives. In this center of inspiration and possibilities, the Spirit has cared for the child who was wounded years ago by the pain of betrayal. Afraid to risk believing in their personal worth and dignity again, Sixes, Ones, and Twos have held their bright and curious Divine Child prisoner in the Repressed Intellectual Center.

Six: The Guardian.   Endurance, the Divine Image for Guardians, is the core of the Intellectual Center. Sometimes the Hebrew name, *Nezah,* is translated as Prophetic Vision or as Victory. The Intellectual Center is the home of vision, true understanding, and original theories. Guided by a clear idea, a person can endure the vicissitudes of life and emerge a victor over odds and obstacles; without such a vision, people perish.

Profiles of their Divine Image of Endurance lie hidden and silent like diamonds in the earth until Guardians—through repeated actions of courage—mine, cut, and polish their inner selves. In this process they discover Real

Beautiful Self, the most priceless gem of all. As navigators of the ancient world were challenged to find a way through the narrow strait between the whirlpool called Charybdis off the coast of Sicily and the large rock called Scylla off the coast of Italy, so Guardians need to navigate their way courageously between conformity to the group, on the one hand, and the stubbornness their opinions can create, on the other. In this process they discover the safe path that only self-awareness and self-discovery can create.

Exercising the courage to trust in the darkness frees the creative curiosity of their minds, expanding confidence in their own thoughts, ideas, and intuitions. In an ever-changing world they become *Stabilizers,* whose ability to believe in self and others strengthens the community and promotes life-giving values.

One: The Achiever. The Divine Image for Achievers is Wisdom (*Hokhmah*). The Intellectual Center yields a penetrating insight into the meaning of all reality, on the philosophical side; on the practical side, it perceives the untapped potential in the things of the world. These qualities combine in inventiveness, discernment, discrimination, and judgment. The Intellectual Center is able to ponder a reality until it gives up its inner secrets, its wisdom.

However, Wisdom will not shout to be heard above the clamoring created by all the demands and half-finished projects in the lives of Achievers. It quietly waits until Achievers come to trust others and life enough to patiently allow the process to unfold as gently as a flower. Thus, they claim the right to give themselves the gift of time to contemplate, reflect, and be alert and open to opportunity. As they begin respecting themselves, profiles of their Divine Image of Wisdom begin to gracefully contour the ground of their being as the bright and curious Real Beautiful Self is set free.

Open, waiting, and watchful, Achievers see the dawn, and the inner resources of love of learning, wonder, and imagination—like the rising sun—enlighten their inner vision and broaden the horizons of possibility with meaning. By marshaling these deeper qualities, Achievers become *Pathfinders* for the human race in their quest for excellence, truth, and practical answers to human questions.

Two: The Helper. The Divine Image for Helpers is Understanding; the Hebrew name (*Binah*) is also translated Intelligence. The natural resources of the Intellectual Center include discovering a clear and true comprehension of all things, fathoming deeply the spiritual level of reality, and reflecting on truth to uncover simple solutions to life's difficulties. The Understanding that proceeds from the Intellectual Center, when properly used, is crystalline and pure—the result of pondering many details until underlying patterns, ideas, and theories are revealed.

However, Understanding will not hustle its way through the crowd of ideas about helping the scores of people who usually occupy the lives of Helpers. Neither will Understanding fight to overpower the public image of being saintly, kind, and helpful that Helpers cultivate. Instead, it invites Helpers to sit humbly on the earth of their own soul and listen to the bubbling springs of life. In this place of interior peace and centeredness, imagination and intuition guide Helpers in sorting out their lives and priorities and discovering the meaning and purpose for their existence.

As profiles of their Divine Image of Understanding begin to emerge in their lives, they discover Real Beautiful Self and come to believe in themselves as persons—to believe they have intrinsic value and dignity as human beings. Touching their self-worth opens their potential for mutual relationship. Becoming *Partners* with people on the journey of life, they face the joys and struggles of their own lives as well as others' with an intelligence that is always sensitive to the human dimension of situations.

Repressed Creative Center

Nines, Fours, and Fives repress the Creative Center. Profiles of the Divine Image of the Father/Mother have been layered into the contours of their lives every time they risked being spontaneous, expressive, or creative. In this center of joy and completion, the Father/Mother God has cared for the child who was wounded years ago by the pain of abandonment. Afraid to risk hoping in their personal value or importance again, Nines, Fours, and Fives have held their playful and adventuresome Divine Child prisoner in the Repressed Creative Center.

Nine: The Preservationist. Presence, the Divine Image for Preservationists, is the core of the Creative Center. Sometimes the Hebrew name, *Shekhinah,* is translated

Immanence or Community. The Creative Center is the home of movement, intent, and energy; through it people accomplish and make their presence felt in the lives of others. Guided by this intelligence, people become both practical and ingenious, realistic and inventive.

In the lives of Preservationists, Presence is cut up into little pieces and scattered among many relationships and activities, none of which have much consequence or purpose except to distract Preservationists from the strength of their true nature. When instead of playing they choose to work diligently at developing self-awareness and meaningful personal relationships, when instead of being affable and easygoing they choose to be goal-oriented, Preservationists discover Real Beautiful Self, whose life has value and who possesses healthy self-esteem.

Through acknowledging these strengths, they can allow others to depend on them, can have confidence in themselves, and can feel that others can be depended upon. In gathering what has been scattered, profiles of their Divine Image of Presence appear in their lives. They discover their gentle power to welcome and receive all without prejudice and to understand comprehensive human truths, and in so doing they discover their new-found identity as *Universalists*.

Four: The Individualist.   The Divine Image for Individualists is Power (*Gevurah*). The Creative Center is the intelligence of resolve, purposefulness, and action. Through it, things happen in the real world. Its love of freedom, capacity to protect and defend, and inventiveness combine to produce, rearrange, and redefine actual realities into new shapes and forms. With the power of creativity, people make the world a better place to live in—more beautiful, more highly principled, more enjoyable, safer, more responsive to human need.

Power is held captive in the lives of Individualists as countless feelings—each stealing strength from the soul through overanalysis and overattachment—become planks of walls, floor, and ceiling of a prison in which Power languishes through lack of use. However, when Individualists choose the serenity of objectivity over the self-indulgence of a totally personal viewpoint, Real Beautiful Self awakens and liberates Power for its true purposes.

Profiles of the Divine Image of Power are etched into the personality as they venture into the midst of life, free to share their newfound gift of hope. As the prison is torn down plank by plank, each piece of lumber is used to build bridges over relationship chasms, shelters for the lonely and despairing, and temples of art, commerce, and spirituality. In these ways Individualists become *Builders* of a new and better world.

Five: The Observer. The Divine Image for Observers is Beauty; the Hebrew name, *Tif'eret,* is also translated Compassion. The Creative Center is the intelligence of both being and doing, of celebrating the wonder of life as well as improving its quality. Through it, both the natural resources and the fruits of the earth are put to practical use for the welfare of humanity. It is the intelligence by which people know how to develop a project stage by stage to create progress.

However, Observers ignore Beauty, preferring the abstraction of logical thought and the antiseptic world of theories and ideas to her more earthy presence. Thus, Beauty has no place to radiate her natural charm and grace, nor can she reflect herself in the things of the world until Observers generously attend to the real world of people and things. With that shift in perspective, Real Beautiful Self awakens and reveals love of and concern for the material world.

Called to investigation of and involvement in that world, Observers come to trust themselves enough to relate spontaneously with others and develop hope in themselves. They become *Explorers,* appreciating and creating beauty and responding compassionately to people and situations.

Escaping the World of In-between

Inevitably, people who long to escape from the absurdity of endless activity and discover a reason for their existence can only *get out* of this meaningless rat race by *going in.* Spirituality is an intrinsic component of every human being that will never cease to vie for our attention. Only through the choice to enter the interior world of soul can we learn to integrate this spiritual reality into the essence of our lives.

Through the course of our lives we've become caught in a dualistic, in-between world that has split us off, divided us from our true selves, from the Divine Source of our life, and from each other. As the Buddhist Dr. D. T. Suzuki observed about Christianity: God against man, man against God; man against the world, the world against man; God against the world, the world against God—funny religion. Unfortunately, the observation holds just as true for the secular society that Christianity in the West has done so much to form.

We've been alienated from the God within and held captive in an illusionary world for so long that we believe the lie that the only reality is the external World of In-between. All the evils of personal and social disintegration, loss of meaning, and violence are the result of our having become, at the very least, far too distant from the Divine Source of life—if not cut off from it altogether.

The way out of this split world is to go within, where we can regain and remember the experience of ourselves as a profile or image of God. Without a personal, immediate experience of the presence of God in our lives, we can't find a meaning for life or discover our destiny, for we can't free ourselves from the World of In-between.

With the focus of the West on the external world, we have lost a sense of the reality of the world within us. Consequently, though some will give lip service to belief in an internal presence of God, the commonly accepted and taught religious belief is that God is transcendent alone. The belief that God is above and beyond the reach of humanity has undoubtedly been the single greatest source of alienation and disconnection from the Source of all life. The corollary of a focus on the God-out-there-somewhere is an undue emphasis on our responsibility to go to God—to make the connection.

By considering human relationships, we can understand the dilemma this puts Western people in. If we were to reach out to someone in friendship over and over again and that person never reciprocated, how long would we continue to set ourselves up for rejection? Similarly, isn't it the ultimate in egocentric illusion to believe that we have enough desire and power to attract a God who has already made the decision to roam the heavens for all eternity?

Of course, any attempt to speak of an infinite, ineffable Other in purely human terms is futile. But we don't speak here of the purely transcendent God who roams the heavens. Our concern is for the God who has been incarnating into the whole of creation since the beginning of time. This is the God whose profile we carry and who lives in the center of the earth of our being.

Thus, the way up to the Transcendent Other is down into the mystic center of our own earth. From this mystic center, this mystic womb, God gives birth to us, and we return the favor by birthing God in the community, in the world. This is the Immanent God of Incarnation—*the One who loves creation.*

Throughout our journey into soul making we've been moving through layer after layer of illusion—layers of mechanical, unconscious living. In reclaiming the strength and beauty of our Repressed Center we build a bridge between the unconscious and conscious, between the exalted realm of spirit and the material world of beauty and life. Over this Great Bridge of soul, of consciousness, the God who lives within is incarnated. Soul consciousness becomes the passageway through which God revitalizes our lives, empowering us to create and maintain balance in our three centers of intelligence.

Through our efforts to restore harmony to our thoughts, feelings, and actions, a new and higher intelligence, the Center of Communion, is born. Even though birth has taken place, this fourth center of intelligence will, for quite a long time, remain as elusive as Chloë's God who lives in the woods. Yet, as we faithfully continue to explore the woodlands of our soul, *we make ourselves accessible to the God who comes to us,* in the words of Chloë, "because you don't go to God, she comes to you."

Through our presence we continue to create a home for Presence, and eventually this home—called the Center of Communion—will become a dwelling place where all who were separated will live as one. In escaping from the World of In-between by living the paradox that the way out is in and the way up is down, we resolve another line of the Enneagram Riddle (see the Introduction): *Then four become one.*

For Personal and Group Work

1. Modern, educated society has a difficult time with belief. On the other hand, many modern commentators lay the ills of our society at the feet of nonbelief. How would you identify and describe the issues in religion that you find nurturing? that you find create alienation?

2. Reflect on and describe your response to the excerpt from Leonard Bernstein's *Mass,* in the section called "The

Problem of Belief," especially the lines "I believe in God,/But does God believe in me?/I'll believe in thirty gods/If they'll believe in me . . . Who'll believe in me?" Does God believe in human beings? How does God express that belief or nonbelief? How do you experience God in this way?

3. How do you respond to the following statements? It's primarily the responsibility of people to gratefully seek God out. It's primarily the responsibility of people to spend time in meditation and reflection, thereby creating the space and opportunity for God to come to them. What are the consequent responsibilities and decisions that flow from your convictions as you answer these questions?

4. How do you respond to the rhetorical question at the end of the section called "A God who believes in us" that says, "Can anyone be more powerful than one who delights in giving power away freely"? Do you believe this statement describes God? How do you believe it could be true in human relationships?

5. Identify the Divine Image, the God within, for your Enneagram type. How do you respond to the description of this profile of God? Identify and describe the ways this profile of God has been contouring the landscape of your personality.

8

Story Power

_____

*There is properly no
history; only biography.*
—RALPH WALDO EMERSON

Nature, Mr. Allnut, is what we were put on this earth to rise above!" Katherine Hepburn as Miss Rose Sayer spoke these words to Humphrey Bogart at a critical moment in the development of their relationship in the movie *The African Queen.*

With that statement, Miss Sayer clearly—though not with the conscious awareness we speak of in this book— defined her boundaries, intentions, and values. In so doing, she opened the secret passageway to the world of soul. After that—through imagination, the voice of intuition, a lot of hard work along the treacherous river, and eventually through surrendering to their own powerlessness—grace, in the form of falling rain, carried the two of them to their destination.

The African Queen is a story about a long river journey toward freedom. Rosie Sayer, sister and companion of a Methodist missionary in central Africa, is left alone when a renegade army patrol burns down the village to which she and her brother have ministered and her brother dies of a broken spirit. She joins Bogart, Charlie Allnut, a Canadian adventurer who owns a small boat named the *African Queen.* They journey down the river both to find freedom and to sink a ship called the *Louisa,* which is stationed in the lake at the mouth of the river. Through their many adventures a friendship and romance develop between them.

At first, however, it was tension that built within each of them and between them. In a confined space and fighting for their lives, they were forced to question old, automatically accepted attitudes and standards. Whenever they reached a comfortable plateau on their journey, the weather and the dangers of the river would create an external tension, testing their ability to overcome obstacles both in the physical world and in their developing relationship.

Soon after experiencing the wild joy of successfully navigating the river, they were captured by the commander of the *Louisa* and once again faced the prospect of losing their lives. By this time, however, they had become soul makers. They had consciously reclaimed their dignity and freedom.

Because their lives had meaning and they possessed some understanding of the why of their existence, they faced their execution calmly, asking the captain to marry them before being hanged. Death held no power over them. Because they had experienced the freedom of being *alive,* they were also free to die.

Throughout the movie, imagination and intuition were intricately interwoven with the triumphant overcoming of obstacles in the outer world. Through imagination they wandered the invisible world of possibilities and found solutions to seemingly insolvable engine failures and overcame obstacles and personality differences. By following the inner voice of intuition at a critical point toward the end of their journey, they chose the only channel that could lead them through a vast grassy swampland into freedom. Learning to listen to and trust the soul's voice of intuition became critical to their survival when a broad physical view of the situation was impossible.

Every imagined possibility and every sensed intuition had to be enacted in the physical world, or the protagonists would never have lived to discover the why of their existence. Life circumstances presented these characters with an opportunity to discover the meaning of *their* lives—not simply the meaning of life in general. Though *The African Queen* can be thoroughly appreciated simply as entertainment, on a deeper, symbolic level it is a story of the journey into soul and a portrayal of soul making.

Finding Your Destiny in Everyday Life

The journey of soul making is a *personal* quest that can't be generalized. Yet, as a quest for life meaning, it is far from myopic. We are continually challenged to learn the secrets of applying the exciting insights discovered in the inner world to the often seemingly mundane routine and tension of daily life.

In the abstract, the idea of discovering personal meaning, destiny, purpose, or the why of our existence can sound terribly exciting. The lived experience, however, is quite different as daily we deal with the reality of irritating relationships, the demands of responsibility, and our own clumsy, often unsuccessful attempts to rise above pettiness. Because our lives seem so ordinary, it's difficult to believe that our efforts—no matter how sincere—could actually be called soul making.

Still, it's precisely in our everyday struggle to become conscious and creatively responsive that we discover practical ways to contribute our growing wisdom to the betterment, the transformation, of the world. Thus, as the magnificent mystery of personal soul making unfolds, a Great Bridge of soul is also being formed in the world.

Soul making takes place in the tension between reconciling our changing inner values with the patterned, unconscious ways we have lived—ways so accurately described by the Enneagram. That tension creates the energy that can free us from the prison of our less-than-human behavior. To *rise above* nature is to *reclaim the beauty, freedom, and fullness of our humanity* from the prison of compulsion—the dungeon of unquestioned and egocentric thinking, feeling, and doing.

Seeing our lives as a series of stories, and learning to tell our stories, is one of the most creative means of soul making that can be released in the life of an individual or a community. Through stories, we develop imagination and intuition and create in ourselves a sense of continuity, a sense of connectedness.

So much of life's wisdom is lost because we lose the stories of our lives. Then, as Sam Keen says, we spend our lives listening to other people's stories in the form of entertainment and often miss the point of stories altogether.[1]

Earlier in this book we wrote about the creative imagination and intuition that rises from the minds of children when they are exposed to fairy tales and how that creativity continues to grow and be released throughout adulthood. Now, however, we are addressing the creative power that is released in individual lives as people remember their lives by remembering their personal stories. As the creative energy of personal story is dispersed into the community, that energy replicates itself over and over, giving life to others. In this process, the collective consciousness rises to a higher level. Thus, another line of the Enneagram Riddle is resolved (see the Introduction): *Then one becomes all.*

The Power of Personal Story

A budding young artist came home from her second grade art class and informed her parents that she had just received the "power of God." More than a little curious, her parents asked her to tell them what she meant. With an impish laugh, the little girl explained, "I don't *really* have the power of God. But my art teacher said when I draw or paint a picture I can create whatever I want—

[1]Sam Keen, "Telling Your Story" (Boulder, CO: Sounds True Recordings, 1987).

whatever I can think in my mind. So it's kinda *like* the power of God."

Reframing our past. In personal story we are free to create or re-create our lives in any way we desire, so it's *like* having the power of God. We can reframe our story, seeing it from a new perspective. With the distance of time, the meaning of important events in our lives changes, and so our telling of them will change. Sometimes we can even see how our story fits into a larger story, a story that comes from the very core of humanity, and then we understand how our lives have divine meaning.

Often we need to tell our stories because we have been locked into stories of neglect, abuse, victimization, and powerlessness from our past experiences. Children are very often victimized and powerless. In the more than twenty years since we began working with people on issues of personal growth and inner healing, we've never met anyone who didn't have some issues of childhood pain that continued to resurface in adult life. Even the best-intentioned, most loving parents can't prevent their children from experiencing the pain of being human.

The good news is that, as adults, we are presented every day with opportunities to rewrite negative childhood scripts, for now we have the power to re-parent that wounded child who still lives within us. Personal story is one of the most powerful tools we have at our disposal to heal the pain of the past, as well as the pain of the present. Through it, we gain a fresh perspective; we see old facts in light of new developments; we discover and rejoice in the gift that has come to us in pain. In re-story-ing our past and present, we are also creating the story of a much happier future, for as the past is healed, new and ever-widening possibilities for the future open.

We can begin the process of re-storying our past and present by looking at the pain of our Original Wound and remembering how the issue of abandonment, be-trayal, or alienation has been a repeating pattern in our life. As we begin to recognize how this initial experience has acted like a magnet, drawing similar experiences to it-self, we can begin to perceive how we unconsciously set ourselves up to continue to be victimized. How did the God who lives in our pain respond to the suffering, for-gotten child who lives within us? That silent experience is also true, and through prayer, imagination, and intu-ition, we can begin to discover a new dimension of the truth of our lives. Once the reality of our deepest self emerges, we can begin to re-member the true story of who we were created to be. With those insights in place, we can begin to use our imaginations to create a new story line for our lives.

Once we catch a glimpse of the mental images and scenes that might also describe our life stories, we're ready to release the flow of creative energy that is like the power of God. Receiving the positive mental images of who we can become is a free gift from the God who loves and believes and lives within. Our efforts to maintain and cherish these positive mental images will slowly start to correct the negative attitudes we've been carrying un-consciously through our lives.

Overcoming negative attitudes. The wisdom of the Enneagram teaches us that our unconscious negative attitudes unleash the greatest destructive and violent energy in our own lives and the lives of others. Some readers will not understand how negative attitudes can have such far-reaching consequences; rather than explain, we'll tell a story.

Early this spring we noticed that a pile of weeds, dry flower stems, grasses, and mud suddenly appeared on one section of the patio. Upon investigation we discovered a small opening in the eaves just above the mess. For several days we watched as two dark-colored birds flitted in and out of the opening with their treasures. We were torn between letting the birds live rent free and raise a family in the attic or finding a way to get rid of them. Because we weren't sure how to tackle the problem of eviction, and because they were rather interesting to watch, we did nothing.

One day Kathy's son came to visit, and we told him about our new nonpaying residents. When he asked what kind of birds they were, neither of us could tell him. Fortunately one was sitting just outside the window on the telephone wire in plain view. When he saw the bird he grimaced and said, "Those are starlings! If you don't get rid of them, you won't even be able to use your patio. They're so aggressive they'll keep diving at your head until you leave—especially if they're raising a family just above you. At construction sites guys dread finding a nest of starlings in the eaves because they'll attack a man so belligerently that he can't even get up a ladder." With that information we suddenly found a way to evict our new tenants. They had not yet laid their eggs, so it was a much easier job than it would have been a few weeks later.

Negative attitudes are like starlings who live in the attics of our minds. They've taken up permanent residence and continue to breed. They attack us (and we attack others) with a vengeance whenever we enter that area of thought and experience. Worst of all, we're letting them live in our minds rent free!

Now, every time you start feeling, thinking, or acting negatively toward yourself or others you can remember the story of the starlings and know that you've just found a nest of negativity that needs to be cleaned out and reclaimed. This is just one example of how we can use the experience of everyday life to begin re-storying our lives. Ordinary experiences that would be quickly forgotten become continuous threads of wisdom, woven into the fabric of our lives through story.

Life, when viewed as an ongoing series of short stories with a common thread and theme, will eventually become our personal sacred wisdom literature that will be passed from generation to generation as we develop the courage to share our stories with others.

Story Telling: Healing Power for Community

Without exception, the most effective teaching technique that can be used to communicate an idea is a story. Stories—especially real-life experiences—bypass the logical, analytical mind and become imprinted in the heart intelligence or Relational Center, the seat of our ego consciousness or self-identity. Not only are stories nonthreatening, but listeners also receive and interpret their message according to the circumstances of their own lives.

Whenever we present a seminar, participants will invariably comment on how deeply at least one of our stories touched them. Even years after having presented a seminar, we'll meet people who tell us how a particular story of ours helped them work through a difficult issue or relationship.

Stories possess a quality of agelessness. A story heard today may communicate a message we desperately need to hear. A year from now, the same story may have an entirely new meaning for us. Because we grow and change, the wisdom relates to our new level of understanding and speaks in a new way to our soul.

Certainly, not every story is going to convey wisdom to every listener, any more than a particular form of music could touch the heart of every listener. Yet, just as music is called the universal language of love, stories of human experience express the universal language of soul.

In chapter 5, we referred to faith, hope, and love as the three power connections between heaven and earth that enlighten and unite a divided universe. Immediately and intuitively, the soul recognizes these golden threads that bring the wealth of the spiritual world into the material realm. Both music and story, then, take on a numinous quality when they convey a truth that flows out of one of the three great virtues.

Whenever stories of faith, hope, or love are shared with others, their truth and wisdom become an eternal echo that lifts the hearts and minds of those who listen, expanding and healing the soul of the community, the soul of the world. Stories of empowerment that continue to encourage others on their journeys unfold in the seemingly uneventful circumstances of people's daily lives. These average stories bespeak the great and magnificent beauty of the human soul and reveal to us all that there is no such thing as an average or ordinary person—only excellent, extraordinary people. The following trilogy of stories are snapshots of three seemingly "ordinary" people.

Brandon's Story of Hope

I (Ted) met Brandon in July 1990. He was a little boy who was just about to turn six. Brandon was as cute and energetic as could be. He was also battling brain cancer. A year before, an ependymoma (a tumor in the ependyma, the membrane lining the ventricles of the brain and the spinal cord) had suddenly appeared in the middle of his brain.

After ten major surgeries and full chemotherapy treatment, he was alive and for the moment looked well, even though he bore the scars of his ordeal—a bald head crisscrossed with incisions and a tubelike ridge on his skull where a shunt had been surgically inserted to drain the two ventricles destroyed by the tumor.

He wasn't out of the woods. His parents, friends, and church community were ever aware that ependymoma can be an aggressive cancer. Cancerous cells can easily be carried through spinal fluid. Once they are lodged in the central nervous system, a new tumor develops and grows quickly, causing vomiting, headaches, and other symptoms. If this course is unchecked, it quickly proceeds to death.

One month later the doctors discovered another tumor, this one embedded in the right hemisphere of the brain. The operation to remove it left Brandon's left side crippled and disfigured. Several months after that episode, an inoperable tumor developed in his neck. This time twice daily radiation to the neck and the head was the therapy, with its consequent nausea and other side effects. The side effects of all the drugs he consumed along the way are too numerous to describe; suffice it to say that though they can prolong and even save life, they do not contribute to the quality of day-to-day living.

Throughout this ordeal, Brandon's continual humor, love of the present moment, and sweetness of spirit kept us all amazed. You couldn't get near him without him impishly pulling your nose or plying you with riddles. Sitting next to me quietly one day watching television, he looked up and smiled, saying, "I love you, Ted."

Yet, he was also honest about his illness. "I know I could die," he told his dad one night in bed. "I don't want to go and be with God." To an interviewer who asked him how he felt about cancer, he replied in a plaintive voice, "I wish I never had this cancer." Once when asked about all the incisions, injections, and blood samples his therapy involved, he volunteered, "I don't like getting poked. It hurts. Wouldn't it hurt you?"

Walking with Brandon, his younger sister, Brianna, and his parents, Brad and Rita, has been a gift to me whose value continues to unfold. As they faced the realities of each day, experiencing and working through wave after wave of grief, despair, anger, and desolation, I stood with them as they climbed over mountains to process their emotions honestly and maintain relationships. Again and again and again, they came back from isolation to one another, to grandparents and family, to friends and church members—to relate, to receive, to give, at times to be hurt and reconciled, to love, and to grow themselves in astounding ways.

After a while, I became aware of the ways I and others intellectualize ongoing traumatic situations in order to escape the pain of them. Brad and Rita chose not to escape that pain. One common intellectualization was a variation on the theme, "You've gotta have hope. This will work out."

The difficulty with those optimistic words was that this family was continually expressing true hope by dealing realistically with daily issues. Laughing or crying when the situation called for it, acknowledging joyful or despairing feelings when they were there, intensely being with the situation and also escaping it with creative "time-outs"—they got through each day, didn't lose their sanity, and didn't lose sight of one another and the people around them. That was real, gritty hope.

For these reasons, when in the early months of 1991 the doctors' prognosis was not hopeful, no one was surprised by Brad and Rita's decision. They had thus far exhausted all therapy that could be administered locally—a person can take only so much chemo, so much radiation, and so many operations to the head. With the hope born of love and desperation, they listened as the doctors described one last, highly volatile procedure—bone marrow transplant.

When they decided to go for it, Brad and Rita knew the cost it involved: They would have to move to Los Angeles for eight weeks. Bone marrow (which grows white blood cells that defend us from disease) would be extracted from Brandon's hip. Brandon would be injected with an almost lethal dose of an agent that would kill cancer cells, but would also kill his bone marrow, and could also kill him. His own extracted bone marrow would be reintroduced into his body to bring the marrow back to life. During the procedure Brandon's already tortured body would suffer painful mouth sores and other distress, and he would have to live in various stages of isolation for 150 days. They also knew the success rate was 50 percent—one out of two patients die either in spite of or because of this procedure.

Brandon had a few low moments during that time. The mouth sores and pain were intense, and the isolation was hard for a six-year-old to take. Yet he was proud that he would be able to go back to school and move on to second grade in the fall because he had kept up with his work.

When the doctors discovered another inoperable tumor a few weeks before Brandon's seventh birthday, we all wept. What a birthday party we had that August afternoon! Everyone came; wonderful gifts were given. Upon opening each gift, Brandon shouted over the hubbub to thank the giver for the present. When his dad commented, "Well, Brandon, it looks like you're the king of the birthday presents." Brandon replied to us all, "I guess that's because so many people love me."

With all the love, all the prayers, all the overcoming of obstacles, we looked at his little body failing every week and wept some more. It was in the fall when the doctors took another look at the tumor and said they had been mistaken—it now appeared to be shrinking and not growing and was probably scar tissue—that it slowly dawned on us what real, hardy hope could accomplish, the kind of hope that feels emotions, works through obstacles, loves life, and cries and laughs in the midst of the worst.

From that moment on, Brandon's body strengthened. At this writing he is alive and getting stronger. His body isn't perfect—his left side is still crippled, he walks with a cane, side effects from radiation and chemotherapy may yet appear—but he is still with us laughing, telling riddles, and loving life every day.

All of us around him who took the opportunity that was offered by walking with him on his journey were strengthened, too. We became dedicated soul makers. Brad and Rita found, among other things, a deepening of intuition that is providing new guidance for the way they live their lives today, and for their plans for tomorrow. I found Brandon reawakening my inner child, the Divine Child who is guiding me in solving the riddles of my life.

We don't know what Brandon's final outcome will be. We do know that, right now, he and many others are living fuller lives for having forged their souls in the crucible of pain with each other and with hope.[2]

Marie's Story of Love

A friend of ours tells of how, from the first moment she understood what it meant to be adopted, she would look into the mirror or at her reflection in a store window and wonder, "Whose face am I wearing?" Although even as a little girl she never voiced that question to anyone, it remained in her mind into adulthood. Thus, after she grew up and left home, she was determined to find her birth mother.

As she began her investigations, she was cautioned over and over by others not to expect acceptance from her birth mother. After all, she was given up for adoption for a reason; by finding her mother, she may be resurrecting unpleasant memories for the woman. Our friend, whom we'll call Marie, had a fairly realistic view of life and people, and so she had no illusions about her birth mother being delighted to have Marie suddenly reappear in her life.

Marie's realistic outlook was indeed a blessing, because the woman she found and identified as her mother

---

[2]Kathy and I chose to dedicate our first book both separately to people we love and together to all who have participated in our Enneagram seminars. My dedication read, "To Brandon, my little friend, whose laughter, love, and vulnerability in the midst of suffering transform my world and teach me the true meaning of life."

wanted nothing to do with the child she had given up years before. She rejected Marie in a most cruel manner, saying that she had made it clear in the hospital that she didn't want her, didn't want to see her, didn't want to even know her sex—this she found out only because she had to sign a release.

"That certainly wasn't a pleasant experience," Marie recounted, "but the important thing for me was that when I looked at her I saw myself. At long last, I knew whose face I was wearing."

During her trip to meet her mother, something else happened that helped to soften the cruelty of her birth mother's response. Marie met her half-brother, who was three years younger than she. "I saw that we both wore different, but similar, versions of the same face. The whole experience gave me a sense of continuity, of history," she recounted. "At last I knew that I came from somebody, that I was a real person and not just hatched on a fence post in some empty field all alone. That realization gave me a lot of peace."

The name Marie that we've given our friend to protect her anonymity wasn't a name we chose at random. From the time she was a child, Marie loved to write and has written many short stories and articles for magazines. "In every story I wrote, I named the heroine Marie," she told us. "I never understood why, but I always loved that name—it was magical for me. I always wished it was my name."

The mystery of her love of that name was resolved when she began the search to find whose face she was wearing. Marie learned that she was born in a Catholic hospital in a large city. Because she was born premature, the sister on night duty baptized the infant shortly after birth. The baptismal name she gave the little girl? *Marie!* Unconsciously, Marie was always connected to her history, for the roots of her first name had grown deep into the earth of her soul.

Everyone who worked on the maternity floor at that time was aware that this newborn infant had been completely rejected. Many took the time to hold and love the child. Yet one can only marvel at the wondrous love that must have flowed into the heart of that newborn baby as an unknown sister held her close, whispering the name that would mysteriously echo in Marie's heart throughout her life! During that lonely night, could that sister ever have imagined that the story of the child she held in her arms, loving unconditionally for a short time, would become a parable of the power of love almost fifty years later?

Through their work of caring for the poor on the streets of Calcutta, Mother Teresa and the sisters of her order have witnessed the incomprehensible healing power that is released as they hold and unconditionally love the sick and dying. Many times Mother Teresa has stated that even for a dying newborn infant, one moment of unconditional love is an eternal act. Because of that earthly experience of love, the child will recognize the Face of Love through all eternity.

If one moment of conscious love will eternally connect the tiniest soul to Love, then Marie's story is probably the most common story ever told. Still, it staggers the imagination to ponder the possibility that our every loving thought, word, and deed could be healing and expanding the soul of the universe until it is *"filled with the utter fullness of God."*

Mildred's Story of Faith

In the early years of World War II, the mother of a large Catholic family struggled with her pain and fear as she helplessly watched her oldest child, a son, enter the military. In her desperation and powerlessness, she turned to the one person she believed could understand her pain. "Mary," she prayed, "I have taken care of him and been the best mother that I knew how to be. Now, I can no longer watch over him. So I entrust him to you—you can do at least as good a job as I have done."

Out of her simple act of faith, a vision of reality took root in her heart that was not to be wrenched from the earth of her being even when faced with the most violent emotional upheaval. Though the mail was slow and letters from her son seemed all too infrequent, this mother continued to write faithfully. One bright day in early September a letter she had written to her son was returned. On the front of it his commanding officer had scrawled the words, "Killed in action August 9th."

Terror pierced her heart like an icy dagger in that moment. Yet, in the silence that followed, her mother's heart somehow reconnected to her faith, her vision, for in a short time she said to her children, "There is more power in heaven than there is on earth. We believed in the beginning, and we believe now." With that, she put the letter high up on a shelf in her closet and went about life as usual.

In October, she received a telegram from the War Department that read in part, "Your son, James, was killed in action August 9." Although her reply was simply, "If we didn't believe it the first time, why would we believe it now?" she constantly needed to face down the demons of doubt and fear with prayer, faith, and the courage to hold on to her vision.

A few months later, the woman was shopping in the small town where she lived. Suddenly she heard someone calling her name and turned to see the local barber waving at her. Having attracted her attention, he shouted, "Mildred, your son's name was read on a list over the radio! He's just been released from a prison camp!" A few weeks later her son, James, arrived home to celebrate Christmas.

The power of that kind of vision and faith not only breathes life, meaning, and purpose into the individual, but that belief continues to be reborn in others—empowering them to believe in and search for their own vision and to journey toward their own destiny. It's the pain, struggle, and joy of this kind of soul making that produces fruit that reseeds itself over and over again in the lives of others. It's always through an individual's journey into the sacred land of his or her own soul that profiles of God—profiles of faith, hope, and love—are eternally etched into the landscape of the community's soul, into the soul of the world.

The wisdom of the Enneagram guides us into the land of our own soul and, in words more suggestive than descriptive, sketches a profile of the God who lives within. Many people have difficulty believing that they carry within themselves a Divine Image. Many have difficulty believing that anything they do or say in the course of their everyday lives could possibly affect the lives of countless people in positive ways. If you are one of those people, look again at the life of the woman in the story.

She lived in a small town all her life, married, and raised a family. There was nothing outstanding or unusual about the way she lived. She never heard of the Enneagram and never knew that the Divine Image she carried was Endurance—also translated as Prophetic Vision or Victory. No one would have been more surprised than she to learn that anything she ever said or did would ever make a difference to anyone outside her own family. She had no way of comprehending that the profile of her Divine Image would continue to create life-enhancing contours in the world long after her death.

Being a rather shy woman, she would probably have been a little embarrassed to think that her life would be used to exemplify the way that *one becomes all*. Thus, it's probably best that she never knew one of her daughters would one day write about the power of her faith, the power of her vision.

Living at a Higher Frequency

Faith, hope, and love are the golden threads that link heaven and earth. They have this power because, in the language of the Enneagram, they each are associated with the higher purpose of one of the three centers of intelligence. Faith raises the Intellectual Center to new heights; hope allows the Creative Center to operate at a higher vibration; and love is the transcendent expression of the Relational Center.

A great difficulty with these three qualities is that people think they can work to have them, to possess them as if they were things to be held or controlled. Indeed, some of us have been taught to work for these virtues, and we were told if we didn't have *enough* of them we weren't working up to our spiritual potential.

More realistically, faith, hope, and love are much larger than any human being. They have *us* much more than we have them. They call the three centers to levels of performance more in consonance with the true beauty of our human nature. Of course, as we have already noted, when centers operate at these higher frequencies, they tend to unite and inform each other. That's why you probably noticed qualities of all three virtues in each of the stories above, even though each focused on one virtue.

Acknowledging that each of these three virtues is associated with a unique center of intelligence further defines and clarifies them for us. Look in any dictionary or thesaurus, and you will see how confused our culture is about all three. Love is often confused with sentimentality and not seen in its strength. Faith and hope are often hopelessly confused with each other; often the very same words—*trust, belief, reliance*—are used to describe them. Why, "faith" is even given as a definition of *hope*, and vice versa.

Faith. True faith raises the vibration of the Intellectual Center. However, lesser versions of faith often are passed off as the real thing. One of them is "magical thinking," the notion that things should work out the way we want them to, just because we want them to. Thus, faith sinks to wishing, and you could interchange the phrases "I believe it is true" and "Wouldn't it be nice if it were true."

On a more logical side, sometimes people are encouraged to "think through" their faith; though it is important for faith to have an intellectual foundation, it's just that— a foundation. When we *believe* that something is true, we can build our thinking on that fact. But the fact isn't the building. Faith must go beyond our intellectual constructs.

True faith—the kind that calls the Intellectual Center to its transcendent functions—is vision. It's seeing the whole picture: not only what can be apprehended through the five senses, as it were, but that combined with all that can be comprehended by intuition, imagination, and spirit, too. Faith is getting the big picture, seeing the true nature of the entire universe we live in. It's seeing all reality and admitting the truth of all reality—agreeable and disagreeable aspects; material, psychological, and spiritual aspects; levels of reality revealed in information, truth, and mystery.

Hope. True hope raises the vibration of the Creative Center. People often confuse it, however, with wishing and wishful thinking. Their idea of having hope is remaining optimistic, even refusing to look at the harsher realities of life though they're staring you in the face.

They'll tell a person who is in the midst of tragedy, "You've gotta have hope," meaning, "Look at the bright side, and don't make me look at reality with you."

True hope—the kind that calls the Creative Center to its transcendent functions—is confidence. It's trust in the universe, so it's built on true faith, which yields an accurate vision of the universe. Because the trust is deep, you can look at, face, and deal with tragedy, pain, and confusion by drawing on an inner stamina. You don't have to look away and be foolishly optimistic when the circumstances call for facing hard realities.

With this attitude, true joys can be fully savored when they come. Having hope means not being afraid of reality, being confident that, through grace, you can handle whatever comes your way. It's knowing that, in a grace-filled universe, you can become big enough, expandable enough, and flexible enough to deal realistically with life. You possess the inner resolve, purposefulness, and drive to keep moving through realities and to discover creative responses to life.

Love. Love raises the vibration of the Relational Center. Often, however, people think of love as a flimsy feeling whose coming and going should direct our relational life. We feel this kind of love one minute and don't the next, and we use these passing sensations as excuses for all sorts of dysfunctional living.

Within certain religious and spiritual circles, love has also been taken to the other extreme. They teach that love among people should always be of the highest form and therefore without feeling, without attachment, simply wanting and working for the best for the other person.

The ancient Greek civilization had a more comprehensive notion of love and saw four major expressions of it. *Filia* is the love within family; *eros* is romantic, sexual, and sensual love; *storgé* is the love of faithfulness, the "for better and for worse," the staying with a person through both bad and good times kind of love; and *agapé* is a love without prejudice or boundary, a love that is unearned but freely given.

One of the greatest obstacles to releasing the power of love—the kind that calls the Relational Center to its transcendent functions—is caused by our dualistic mentality. Some would say love is taking care of myself and mine; others would argue that love calls us not to be involved in self but to be involved in others, not self-centered but other-centered. Love can't be an either-or proposition, or even a both-and dialogue, for true love transcends all and wears myriad faces. The only consistent description possible for love is that love always unifies.

Love unites me with my deepest self and unites my deepest self with others. Love unites earth and heaven, and it incarnates heaven on earth. Love is the passionate power that gives to self and others, without counting the cost, and receives from self and others without examining the price. Love transcends division, mends what is broken, and heals what is wounded. It is a passionate power that cannot be contained.

For Personal and Group Work

1. Everyone has a severely restricted ability to access and develop one of the three great virtues necessary for a healthy and balanced life. Reflect on the wound in your Repressed Center and the virtue connected to that wound. Can you identify ways that this virtue has been the most elusive and difficult to understand in your life experience? Reflect on the virtues related to your Dominant and Support Centers. Can you identify the ways that these virtues have strengthened you on your life journey?

2. Using your strongest virtues as guiding themes, tell something of your life story to another person. If that's not possible for you, take time to write a part of your life story in your journal. Share or write it in the most honest, yet positive way possible.

3. Whether you view your past as positive or negative, what strengths did you develop in growing up that continue to empower you in your adult life? How did the liabilities you experienced in childhood propel you to develop strengths?

4. Using imagination and listening to the voice of intuition, how might you build a better future using those strengths as cornerstones?

9

World Soul Making

***

*Someday when [human beings] have
harnessed the winds, the waves, the
tides and gravity, they will harness for
God the energies of love. And then, for
the second time in the history of the
world, [humanity] will have
discovered fire.*
—PIERRE TEILHARD DE CHARDIN

The Enneagram teacher John G. Bennett used to say, "Books are like road maps, but there is also the necessity of traveling." Wisdom is enticing, and reading wisdom is exhilarating, but let's not mistake good emotions for the reality they are meant to lead us toward. Unless wisdom creates understanding—unless we allow knowledge to influence our being—the point of reading wisdom will be lost on us.

Reading a book about soul making, therefore, is one thing, but the process of making soul is moving forward in transformation in our daily life. It's forging a soul of quality, integrity, goodness, and beauty in a world and in relationships where differing values create tension that stretches and develops our souls. In these situations it is important to remember the wisdom of the Enneagram: don't waste your energy in negative thinking and negative emotions; instead, use your energy to achieve the higher purpose of balancing all three centers of intelligence. Living with this kind of intentionality will yield the transcendent fourth Center of Communion.

In making positive choices, we discover something intrinsic to the process of soul making: if it remains a purely internal experience, it will soon wither and die, for soul makers are entrusted with bringing the sacred art of compassion into the world.

Unless we bring the fruit of our inner work to bear upon the world, our inner work becomes lifeless, and our vision is impaired by cataracts of illusion. Part of becoming a person fully alive is learning to relate to others in ways that will set them free, not only personally but also in the wider realm of justice and equality. Creating internal unity and an external community of relationships enables us to develop the virtues that empower us to build a healthy world community. This is the crowning action of soul making.

Though the beginning of the journey is indeed personal, it is a type of personal approach with which many people today are unfamiliar. It's not making lists of what is wrong or right about us; it's not the self-contemplation that excludes others and leads to "navel-gazing." Soul making can on the surface appear to be that kind of myopia only because the world has lost contact with the power and life that rises out of the ground of consciousness.

In chapter 2 we wrote that, due to the banishment of even the concept of soul (as separate from spirit) in Western culture, the value of healthy feminine qualities—like personal knowledge, experience, emotion, and treasuring the stories of our own and others' lives—have all but disappeared under a cultural reducing glass. In this book we have attempted to take the reducing glass away from the feminine soul so that we can perceive it, understand it, experience it, and find sources of renewal in it, both individually and interrelationally.

The Enneagram, as a system that assists us in understanding ourselves and our lives, propels us around and through myriad barriers—barriers that have led us into the detours that have prevented us from examining ourselves in depth. At first using our natural fascination with ourselves and our personalities and later using hard-hitting truth about how we behave and why, Enneagram wisdom leads us past illusions of who we are, faithfully guiding us toward an accurate, breathtaking vision of the person we can become. As we gratefully welcome the divine action of grace and cooperate with it through hard work, profiles of the divine begin to form contours on the panorama of our personality and of the world.

Now, in this last chapter, in order to address our topic of world soul making adequately, we must direct our energy to the masculine—both to its inner expression, the spirit, and to its outer expression in the world.[1] In doing

---

[1]See note 5 in chapter 1 about our use of the terms *masculine* and *feminine*—namely, that we are using them in the abstract and not in reference to male and female human beings.

so, we must take from before our eyes the cultural magnifying glass that has both exaggerated and disfigured masculine expression in the West for centuries.

Further, we must penetrate beneath the surface of the obvious signs of evolution in our society to perceive and understand the emerging partnership and union between a *new masculine* consciousness and a *new feminine* consciousness. This partnership will characterize and initiate a new era.

The subject of world soul making is by definition both personal (therefore feminine), because of its inner focus on individual soul consciousness, and transpersonal (therefore masculine), because of its outer focus on world soul consciousness. Thus, world soul making is about how, in the words of the Enneagram Riddle, *all become One,* how all rejoin with the Center of being, not losing but rather heightening their individuality.

The Enneagram does not leave us in peace until we address ourselves directly to this complex issue, for Enneagram wisdom says that our collective attitudes create society. At every step of our evolution as individuals we express ourselves in society. Our work and our energy create both individual lives and community life, forming personal and cultural excellence or decadence. In examining both the personal and the transpersonal dimensions of our existence, we search to understand the individual and collective future toward which we are being irresistibly drawn—a vortex through which a new cultural and spiritual epoch will spiral into the twenty-first century.

Developments in the twentieth century in areas such as politics, economics, philosophy, and theology tell us that the decisions of individuals and groups have been gathering momentum; the rate of change has increased so much that commentators agree this century has seen more change than the six hundred centuries of civilization before it put together. Because with each decade the rate accelerates even more, it is not unreasonable to say we are being propelled into a new era.

What will this post-postmodern era look like? The answer to that question may seem to be impossible to intuit, let alone to formulate in words. Yet, the truth is that this answer already exists, and every human being carries a part of it in his or her mind, heart, and body, ready to be expressed and incarnated in society. As all the individual pieces are assembled, they will enflesh a new culture.

The issues on the forefront of human concern today—prejudice, violence, family values, health, education, drug dealing, the economy, and the disintegrating integrity in politics and business—and the way every person responds in thoughts, feelings, and actions to these issues—are the force that is creating our future. It is apparent that we are living in exciting and perilous times.

These cultural undercurrents have been intuited by prophets as diverse as Carl Jung, Dag Hammarskjöld, Pierre Teilhard de Chardin, Martin Luther King, Thomas Merton, and Mohandas Gandhi, to name a few. It is not unusual for cultural giants to be able to see beneath and beyond the surface of contemporary events. What is especially intriguing is that not one of them had a pessimistic attitude;

instead, each exuded confidence in his unique vision of the future.

Further, their diverse worldviews held a common spiritual perspective that included two profound attitudes: forgiveness, and love for people. If their lives and experience are to be taken seriously, the spirituality of love and forgiveness holds the power to take an individual soul, pry it loose from its little world and egocentric concerns, and, by many small steps of personal transformation, expand it to embrace the world and its destiny—our destiny.

Because each of us possesses the ability to develop the power of perceiving the unseen—the underlying currents that presage the birthing of a new era—we are compelled to make a choice for or against individual soul making. A choice *for* it will take humanity one giant leap forward. Composed of many small steps, this giant leap will propel us into world soul making.

The Challenge to the Old Masculine Mentality

The masculine component is what turns soul making outward to affect the world. However, to accomplish this goal, masculine consciousness must first escape the disfiguring cultural magnification to which it has been subjected for centuries. That is why everywhere in our culture the forces of the old masculine approach—symbolized by the Old Patriarch—are being challenged by a new expression of masculinity that uses its strength to support and empower the community.

The Old Patriarch.   The Old Patriarch is the magnification and distortion of true masculine qualities. It's the
masculine weighted with the ponderousness of self-importance; it's strength and logic without the tempering of
relationship. Suffering from the diseases of old age—
blindness, excessive love of the past, and the irascibility
whose source is senility—the Old Patriarch flails around
in the halls of power trying to repress and destroy what
can no longer be controlled.

This mentality loves the rigidity of law, the power of
hierarchy, and the tyranny of repression. It has long oc-
cupied the throne in institutions of authority, preroga-
tive, and domination—whether in politics, government,
church, education, or corporation.

The difficulty is that the old ways die hard. The institutions of politics, government, church, education, and the
corporate world are still easily controlled by the Old Patriarch's mentality. People involved in these institutions are
often enmeshed in them because their own interests are
being served—a motivation unconscious but nonetheless
real. Consequently, not having reflected on their inner lives
and the values that proceed from them, they may be
shocked into reevaluating their position. If the Old Patriarch
mentality possesses their minds completely,[2] they respond

---

[2]In truth, it often does. In *When Society Becomes an Addict,* Anne Wilson Schaef describes a similar way of thinking as being perpetrated by
four myths: that it is the only system that exists, that it is innately superior, that it knows and understands everything, and that it is possible to be totally logical, rational, and objective (San Francisco: Harper
& Row, 1987, pp. 7, 8). This kind of thinking actually possesses the
mind and becomes addictive.

with ever-growing layers of rationalization and manipulation, group-think and double-speak, and mottoes that thinly veil hidden agendas.

In the public arena, we see men and women who are learning the lessons of this struggle the hard way—in front of cameras and microphones. The more fortunate (in terms of public humiliation) are the hollow heroes whose fifteen minutes of fame cause them quickly to sink into obscurity as the heat of truth melts them like chocolate bunnies in the sun.

The less fortunate are those who are elected or appointed to office or who gain the lasting attention of center stage through personal achievement. If the rigidity of the Old Patriarch possesses them, these people must continually reinvent themselves and defend causes that more and more rapidly appear ridiculous to the nonenmeshed onlooker. This foolishness is least obvious to the ones who express it, however; being enmeshed in the system that creates it, they have only one reference point, which happens to be this rigid way of thinking.

Those of us who live more private lives are not off the hook, though. We, too, get to have our crack at outdated and rigid thinking, feeling, and behaving. That the Old Patriarch mentality still wields power in individual lives is obvious to anyone who knows about demanding instead of relating, commanding instead of explaining, insisting on one's own way instead of being open to a new perspective.

Every time we lose our temper, tear down a new idea, or devalue the dignity of another individual, we give power to the Old Patriarch mentality among us. The Old

Patriarch has no respect for individual autonomy, thinking for oneself, or expression of honest emotion; whenever we witness the degrading or eroding of these values, we witness the rise of the Old Patriarch mentality again.

Signs of the Old Patriarch's thinking can be seen everywhere in the West: attitudes of absolute control, war, and repression; of logic without emotion, science without evaluation, and objectivity without relationship; of creating enemies and then conquering them, overcoming obstacles through technological advances regardless of their effect on people or larger systems, and greed. Foundational as they are to the ethos of Western civilization, more and more these attitudes are being challenged. It may be easier to identify challenges to this approach in events of recent years. Yet, if we peer into the history of this century, we'll discover that the ground was being prepared for this struggle decades ago.

The challenge.   The strength of the new masculine consciousness, symbolized by the Ageless Hero—the vital man, the grounded man, the green man—is fertility, playfulness, cultivation and protection of the earth, and equalitarian partnership with the feminine, without being engulfed by it or demanding its slavish obedience.[3]

------

[3]The new masculinity can't be expressed by the Old Patriarch, but neither does the image of the Youth as Puer Aeternus, or Eternal Boy, as presented in contemporary psychological literature, express him well. The Old Patriarch, or Senex, is rigid and severe; the Puer is not grounded or real in its approach. Neither portrays what is now happening.

Thus we speak of the Ageless Hero who has the qualities of both youth and maturity; this mentality places its vitality at the service of the

The point that must preface any investigation of the new masculine is that new masculine consciousness cannot exist without new feminine consciousness, nor the new feminine without the new masculine. Part of the newness of each is its desire for equal partnership with and respect for the other. The relationship that results excludes old cultural attitudes that have governed the masculine-feminine dialogue—like one overwhelming the other, one manipulating the other, or one being magnified and the other diminished in relation to the other.

Masculine consciousness itself is about spirituality (as we defined spirit in chapter 1) and about achievement in the world. The new masculine consciousness is vigorous, intelligent, and alert. In the image of the Ageless Hero, this awareness both inspires to idealism and inaugurates innovations of both a playful and a revolutionary nature.

The struggle in our society between these two expressions of masculinity is played out daily. For every move inspired by the new masculine consciousness comes an equal and opposing tactic from the Old Patriarch. Yet the youth, vitality, and ingenuity of the new masculine consciousness seems irrepressible as it discovers yet a new way to unfurl the banner of honesty, sincerity, and truth—

---

community and is able to be in lasting, committed partnership with the new feminine consciousness emerging today. With this name we hope to convey a unity of qualities from the four major masculine archetypes: the Father and the Youth, the Warrior and the Sage. Further, we specifically reject the shallow cultural definition of Hero as a warlike person who strives interminably, conquers, and takes a totally exterior focus. The basis for our understanding of the term comes more from Joseph Campbell's richly researched classic *The Hero with a Thousand Faces* (Princeton, NJ: Princeton Univ. Press, 1968).

both because it is inspired by the Divine Child within and because it is in relationship with the new feminine.

All of this, of course, is speaking in the abstract. In no single human being does all of this new awareness continually converge. However, with the support of community and the strength of individual soul making at their core, more and more women and men are giving expression—even if it is sometimes fleeting—to this new way of living.

The New Masculine Mentality and the New Union

World soul making is the appointed task and goal of the union of the new masculine consciousness in partnership with the new feminine consciousness. This new mode of being is expressing itself in both men and women at an accelerating rate as this century and millennium conclude. Before we can explore this new union, however, we will need to take a closer look at the individual and cultural evolution of masculine awareness today.

The Ageless Hero.   The masculine consciousness of the Ageless Hero proposes ideas that are fresh and invigorating. It introduces concepts that cause people to take a new look and, with an air of openness, declare, "We don't have to keep on doing things in the same old, worn-out ways, especially when they're hurting more people than they're helping, or when they no longer apply to the evolving human intellect." This new energy breaks down walls of oppression erected under the solid- ified power structures of the Old Patriarch's institutions and lifts the weights of repression—all to create room for something new.

The challenge is not getting caught in *opposing* the Old Patriarch, for this is the hidden trap that the old, rigid system has always set: to drain people's creative energy and vitality by continually having to define what they are against. Such battles may at first sound important and appear to be righteous, moral causes, but in truth they are another form of enmeshment that distract us from our true goal of building something new.

Enneagram wisdom teaches that nothing positive can come from something negative, and the "against" men- tality is a negative mentality. Thus, to maintain the in- tegrity of the new masculine consciousness symbolized by the Ageless Hero, we must concentrate on *proposing* new ideals and *freely investing* positive, creative energy for the sake of building an era that will be life-giving for all.

One expression of the Ageless Hero is found in love for Mother Earth. Embracing the earth, healthy masculine strength will be expended to cultivate and protect, to re- pair and restore what has been defiled and raped. In union with the feminine, creation will be reconsecrated, blessed, and celebrated. Imbued with a mystical aware- ness, scientific knowledge and technological expertise will be brought to bear on the air, lands, and water that have been ravaged through greed.

Like Icarus, the consciousness of the Ageless Hero soars into the sunlight of spirituality, and also like Icarus, its wings, formed by human ingenuity, will melt if it soars so high it becomes disconnected from the shadow and heated with the light of more truth than it can handle. Yet, the healthy masculine can lead humanity on the spiritual adventure into the uncharted realms of idealism and mysticism. Keen insight and interest in ideas and investigation give birth to a new and ever-changing vision that inspires people to dream, to hope, and to work for renewal.

The spirit of the Ageless Hero inspires new concepts, empowers individuals to grow in strength and freedom, and gratefully contributes to the common good through periods of selfless service. Thus, we can look for the fearless confrontation of emotional and sexual abuse in the family and the workplace, therapies that support people in naming and facing down shame, and volunteer systems in communities and churches that create connection and trust among people as examples of the new masculine consciousness.

The spirit of the Ageless Hero is experienced in families where men and women in partnership nurture, discipline, and teach their children to walk in the ways of honesty, love, and compassion. It appears whenever truth is preached with the love that flows from personal experience and whenever honor and the common good prevail.

The new union. The masculine consciousness of the Ageless Hero, in union with the new feminine, is afoot whenever and wherever repression is cast off and the values of personal freedom and responsibility prevail in society.

This new and creative union will begin to become visible in the world as individual, national, and global concerns shift into alignment, as political systems are reformed to establish in law that equality of all people which is indelibly written in nature, and as governments unite to lay the foundations of interrelationship and peace rather than selfishness and war.

Although no single person, organization, or movement continually and purely expresses this kind of energy, each expression, no matter how fleeting, etches another contour of Divine Image into the landscape of the world soul. Through the emerging union of masculine and feminine, a *temenos*—a sacred space or mystic center—is forming. From this sacred *temenos,* divine and human energy will mingle and flow into the world to transform and revitalize the whole of creation.

World Soul Making and the Enneagram

The broad wisdom that undergirds the Enneagram continually communicates age-old truth in the new, yet practical ways that are needed by today's society. Rather than presenting us with rigid or simplistic answers to the probing, poignant questions that rise out of human experience, this wisdom presents life principles, indicates directions, and points out common stumbling blocks on the path. It is then every individual's right and responsibility to choose how far in and how far out he or she is willing to go.

The question is, How big do we want our own soul to be? Big enough to be involved in making the soul of the world? Like that of a tree, our trunk can only grow as tall and our branches spread as wide as our roots grow deep. If the roots stop growing, the whole tree is weakened and susceptible to disease, and one day a storm will uproot it. Similarly, the masculine consciousness in us that works to affect the world must be balanced by a feminine consciousness that pushes us deep into our own inner work. Otherwise, the winds of change will uproot us one day, for we will have no depth.

Our roots are our connection to our spiritual heritage. The work of forgiveness and love feeds our roots and binds us to the source of vital nutrients for the growth of our soul. Clinging to offenses rots the roots of the tree. Forgiveness leads to understanding, which nourishes the tree. Failure to forgive is raping the land of your own soul.

The new feminine and the new masculine consciousness are challenging us all to strengthen and stretch our souls so that we might make the soul of the world and give birth to the new era we see coming with the twenty-first century. How do we participate in this great adventure? What are the steps we need to take? Again, the Enneagram is our sure-footed guide on our quest to understand, respond, and cooperate with these converging forces in the universe.

The steps toward transformation are simple, earthy, humble. Those who seek a grand or flashy recipe for greatness had best look somewhere else. However, in describing them as separate steps, we create both clarity and confusion: clarity because we can understand each phase distinctly, and confusion because steps imply one must be completed before another can begin.

In real life, such is not the case. Often several steps are occurring simultaneously. Sometimes we reach way ahead of the step in which we are living and, for a moment, touch a more advanced realm. Though such experiences are meant to give us hope—to show us what could be ours if day-by-day we did our inner and outer work—they do not indicate we have *reached* that step. We reach a step when we consistently live by its values.

Thus, by outlining steps we do not mean to indicate that a person has to achieve all the goals of one in order to proceed to the next. We simply want to shed whatever light this wisdom can on our experience and to offer a way to see past our experience to what we can become with grace and hard work.[4]

Waking Up

As the Enneagram faces us with ourselves, we realize we've never faced ourselves realistically before. We are not conscious at all. We're psychologically and spiritually asleep, and the Enneagram simply contains the potential of waking us up.

---

[4]Throughout this entire section, we have relied on Maurice Nicoll's analysis of this issue. See his *Psychological Commentaries on the Teaching of Gurdjieff and Ouspensky* (Boston: Shambhala, 1975), esp. vols. 2, 4, and 5. The specific applications to the all-encompassing shattering of egocentricity, however, are our own insights.

Waking up is not easy, however. Patterns of egocentric thinking and feeling that previously were unconscious rise into the light; behaviors that in the past both mystified and embarrassed us now become understandable. If in this first step of world soul making you let the Enneagram work on your self-image—allowing the wisdom that proceeds from knowing which type you are to come into you and affect your being—you see your unpleasant side more clearly along with your gifts.

At this initial point, people easily get caught up in self-blaming, on the one hand, and in self-justifying, on the other. They get down on themselves for being whatever number they are, thinking it's the worst kind of person in the world to be. At other times, they look at themselves and justify their many failures at becoming conscious by pointing to their positive qualities, which, for the moment, have arrested their attention.

In truth, however, both attitudes are a waste of our time and energy, for they arise out of our egocentricity. Thus, when they occur, we notice them, turn from them, and seek a more even-handed perspective.

Self-observation

In the next step of world soul making, we work at objective observation of our interior and exterior states. Within we make an important psychological step—we divide our sense of self into two, the observing self and the observed personality. We begin to see how much our lives are at the mercy of this personality, which is described by our Enneagram type, and how mechanically it operates.

However, simultaneously, we maintain an even keel—neither blaming nor justifying but simply seeing and admitting the truth of who we are today. It seems like a small thing, but it isn't—it isn't a little thing to accomplish, for it takes great discipline not to blame or justify; and it has no small effect on our being. Self-observation expands our self-awareness to include information about ourselves we don't always find it pleasant to accept.

Receiving that information is painful; welcoming it at first seems impossible. Some people are so thrown by the experience that they don't recover, and they keep the Enneagram's powerful wisdom about their own human nature at arm's length.

Acknowledging your Enneagram type explains all kinds of hidden negative emotions. Each of us has his or her favorites; they're feelings like anger, envy, or self-pity or traits like being easily offended or too ready to judge other people. Negative emotions draw us into compulsion and produce egocentricity. Totally engaging, they are like subpersonalities that take over our identity. Every time one shows up, we say, "I," to it—for example, we say "I am angry at you" or "I am offended at that."

Thus, we allow the sacred energy of our Real Beautiful Self to be used up by inferior and negative parts of ourselves. For, in truth, *I* am much deeper and more real than any negative emotion.[5]

---

[5]We first wrote of the real beautiful self in every person and its relation to positive and negative emotions in chapter 5 of *What's My Type?*

It's as if each one is like a lens through which all the energy of our personality is focused. Thus, we live with the illusion of being a unified individual, but the ordinary sleepwalking person is really many different *I*'s, and the emotion we express at any given moment is not the true person but a distortion of truth—it obscures our real selves.

Disidentifying from Negative Emotions

In the next step of world soul making you come to see that you are not your Enneagram type, you are you. Your Enneagram type is the mechanical and often self-destructive way you express your own sacred energy, but you don't need to waste your energy that way. You can disidentify from your negative emotions and discover a deeper you than you've ever experienced before.

How do we normally handle negative emotions? We welcome them. We let them control our thinking and feeling. Without realizing it—and feeling it's as natural as breathing—we invite negative emotions to take up permanent residence with us, and then we wonder why we have so little energy for positive things and why our lives are dull, depressing, or flat. In other words, we are letting the "starlings in the attics of our minds" live there rent free.

What would you do if you saw the gossipy neighbor who lives down the street come to your door? Would you invite him to come in for a cup of coffee and spill his negativity all over your kitchen floor? Would you let him stay long enough for his negative attitudes to cascade into your dining room? living room? bedrooms? basement? That's what we do with negative emotions. Finally, they're so familiar that we say to our free-loading guests, "Why even go home? Why leave at all? I've got a spare bedroom. Why not live here all the time with me?"

What would happen if we refused to welcome them? What would happen if when the gossip knocked at your door you didn't answer? He would probably knock over and over again, but finally he would walk away.

Refusing to welcome negative emotions means disidentifying from them. We identify with negative emotions when we say "I" to them and let them control us; we say, "I am angry" or "I am hurt" and identify ourselves with these feelings. We pretend the negative emotion is us and allow it to direct our energy, thus obscuring our real selves. When we experience a negative emotion, of course it's important to acknowledge it; not letting go of it is the problem. Disidentifying from negative emotions means differentiating between negative emotions and our real selves and remembering who we really are.

Identifying with a negative emotion is like having an octopus on your face. It distorts your perception and your perspective. You can't see much if there is a big blob obscuring your vision and distracting your attention. You pry free the octopus of negative emotion tentacle by tentacle by remembering who you are—"I am not this negative emotion, I am I, I am mystery, I am child of God, I am positive, creative, and free"—and therefore seeing that the negative emotion is not you. You and it are different, and there is space in between. That space is sacred, for into that space Divine Wisdom can come.[6]

By admitting we have negative emotions and disidentifying from them, we begin to notice a salutary effect. We become more at ease with ourselves, more comfortable living our own lives. These are the first steps of forgiveness; they are forgiveness of self. Forgiveness creates room for real emotions.

Real emotions are positive, for only these effect the goal of an emotion—to express our Real Beautiful Self and connect us with others, the universe, and God. They are gifts; we cannot create them. What the Gospels identify as the Holy Spirit are expressions of positive emotions. If through self-forgiveness we create room within ourselves, we will begin to experience the gift of healthy self-love. It's particularly healthy because it happens in the presence of all our faults and weaknesses.

Recognizing and disidentifying from our negative emotions is ultimately an act of love for ourselves, and it is the only basis for receiving love from others. When this solid base of confidence is securely in place, we are well on our way to world soul making.

Canceling Internal Accounts

Self-forgiveness expands our hearts to forgive others. We can love others to the degree we love ourselves. Thus, this step in

---

[6]For a fuller description of this way of thinking, see *What's My Type?* p. 147, where we call it the Litany of the Real Beautiful Self.

world soul making, canceling internal accounts, is an outward movement, just as the previous ones were inward. Again, the Enneagram is our guide as it describes to us not only our own personality type but other people's as well.

> *In tellin' you this story of the infamous nine*
> *It's easy to see we're all really fine*
> *One pattern no better, one pattern no worse*
> *Each one a blessing, never a curse.*[7]

We look around ourselves and, now able to understand *why* other people do what they do through the knowledge that the Enneagram gives us, we find that our forgiveness for them can grow, too. The nine patterns show us how we're different but equal—all equally strong and weak, gifted and scarred, and valuable to self, others, and society. Understanding other people from the perspective that they are expressing a type, a pattern of behavior, can tame our violence and help us to receive their giftedness more graciously.

Of course, if we keep this information outside us personally, the Enneagram will at first have the opposite effect: we may disdain people who are different from us or use this powerful information to try and get what we want from them. People who treat this wisdom in such a fashion, however, find it soon dies in them and is of

---

[7]From "The Enneagram Rap" by Kathleen V. Hurley, © 1992 Enneagram Resources, Inc.

no further use. Worse, they run the danger of receiving enough wisdom to inoculate them against the "disease" of transformation.

Internal accounts.   Intuitively we know that by taking this knowledge inside us we will lose the basis for our self-justification and self-righteousness, because it forces us to look at our internal accounts. We all count the offenses others commit against us, because whatever we blame as not making our lives easier we tend to personify. I don't get angry at the pothole in the road but at the people I think should fix it. I don't get angry at the crack in the foundation of my house but at the real estate agent who sold the house to me.

Internal accounts are made by the negative *I*'s in us that feel we've got our rights, that others owe us something, that others are in debt to us. We keep accounts inside ourselves against anyone who ever offends us. If you don't believe it, think of the last argument you had and how soon you brought out your list of all the things that person had done to offend you. You had been keeping accounts.

As long as we keep internal accounts we don't have time, interest, or internal room to reach a new understanding. We're too busy listing all the ways others should change to have any time left for work on ourselves. Furthermore, we see no need to work on ourselves, because everyone else is to blame.

Internal accounts lead to violence. As we identify with all the negative emotions toward other people that our internal accounting creates, we become more and more hostile toward them, and we seek revenge. Revenge is sweet, but work on ourselves is not.

Loving people who are different from me.   Forgiving others is work on ourselves, and forgiveness creates understanding, which opens the door to more forgiving. Far from being sentimental, forgiving means canceling a debt, writing off an account from one's own internal list.

The Enneagram assists us by leveling the playing field. The other person is not the only one who is compulsive and destructive; so am I. When I understand what goes on inside another person to create these dysfunctional patterns, I have the choice and the power to forgive.

Thus, if we allow the Enneagram to work inside us, we realize that others aren't out to get us; they are just like us, and we are like them. Maybe the way they express egocentricity differs radically from our own, but we are all egocentric, are easily caught in negative emotions, and have difficulty truly caring for others.

At this point of recognition we have to face ourselves with the question, Can I give to others the gift I always want—a little room to be myself without someone looking over my shoulder ready to nitpick or criticize? Or, to put it more simply, Can I learn to love people who are different from me?

In this context, we see a second important purpose for working on the self-forgiveness and healthy self-love that is the goal of waking up. True self-love makes room in me for something good, positive, and creative to happen; it doesn't fill me up with myself, as some people fear it will.

In truth, it's self-blaming and self-justifying that preoccupy me with myself in endless mental searching.

Loving others as they are means accepting their faults and virtues as a package deal, just as we come to accept ourselves that way. Thus, love is a gift. A little more unity is created in the world—internal unity is now expressed in unity with another person. Making room inside us for something new to be born is a continual process that at times can be inspiring, but most of the time it feels like scratching our way inch by inch through a wall of mud.

Resolving a year-long struggle. Several years ago Kathy and I (Ted) had the most difficult time we have ever had in our relationship. For close to a year, we couldn't say or do a thing that wasn't somehow offensive to the other and/or easily misinterpreted. Finally, one July night I decided we would get to the bottom of the situation, once and for all.

I went to Kathy's house, and we sat on the deck, spewing out all our internal accounts—the arguments and hurt feelings that had accumulated for many months. I don't know how long I stayed, but I do remember that when I came the moon was on my left, and when I departed the moon was setting on my right.

Somewhere about three-quarters of the way into this marathon session, we had spent all our arguments but felt none the better for it. Finally I said to Kathy, "You know what your basic problem is? You don't know how to be a good friend to me." Quick as a flash she retorted, "You're not a very good friend either."

There we were. Stuck. Twenty minutes passed, all in silence but with our minds racing. Finally, I began to think about the Enneagram and how Kathy is a Three and I am a Four. For Threes, friends are people who will see what needs to be done, get up, and work shoulder to shoulder with them to accomplish a task; for Fours, friends are people who will sit down with them, share their feelings, and allow them to do the same. Realizing this, I began to laugh. When Kathy asked why I was laughing, I responded by telling her what I had been thinking.

"So, no wonder we don't think we're good friends to each other," I concluded. "You're waiting for me to stand up, and I'm waiting for you to sit down."

Was the problem really that simple? Yes. Was it that easy to solve? Of course not. We had come to a deeper understanding of each other and our relationship, to be sure. Yes, many of the problems of the previous months became perfectly clear as we looked at them through the lens of this little formula. We began to see how we had been pushing each other's buttons all this time by not reading and honoring the other person's value system.

But that's just seeing the problem. Solving the problem meant we had to move into the next step in world soul making.

Balancing Centers

Solving problems, whether inside ourselves or in relationships, means doing our own inner work. In the language of the Enneagram, that means, at first, balancing centers.

In the story just told, Kathy's wanting me (Ted) to see what needs to be done, get up, and work with her shoulder to shoulder to accomplish tasks meant that I had to develop my Repressed Creative Center, the center of doing. That was hard work. No task ever appears as important as a personal conversation, for example, if you're a Four like me. But that's the illusion. Developing a healthy relationship required that I first confront my illusions and see them for what they were. Then I had to make the agenda of the Creative Center more truly my own. Doing so released the true gifts and strengths of my Dominant Relational Center to be used in a balanced and free way to create relationship.

Similarly what Ted was asking me (Kathy) to do was to acknowledge my personal feelings and his, and to see the value of sharing feelings with each other. That meant developing my Repressed Relational Center, the center of emotion, which for me was no small accomplishment. I remember at times pulling myself from tasks and agendas and forcing myself to listen and to speak in a personal way. But I had to confront the illusion of Threes, the illusion that you can't rest and do superfluous things (like share feelings) till all your work is done. To grow as a person and enter the world of personal relationship that I both dreaded and longed for, I had to confront the illusions created by overemphasizing the importance of my ideas and accomplishments. With those truths apparent, I was free to begin choosing and struggling with the values that lay hidden in my Repressed Relational Center.

This part of the journey into world soul making can initially be the most difficult, for though we have let information into ourselves in the previous steps, it is here that we begin to recognize how big the task is and how long it will take. True, balancing centers in one situation (like the one just described) has its effects in other aspects of our lives, but it's amazing how we find pocket after pocket of hidden resistance to dealing with our real issues.

Another difficulty at this point is that we find the demons of self-negation can be overwhelming. Now, all the ways we've learned to deny our own goodness and affirm our weakness come to haunt us. At this point, we each in our own way easily revert back to negative attitudes like self-pity, blaming others, and abdicating responsibility for change. None of these stumbling blocks, however, need become blockades. The forgiveness and love we found in the first two steps of this journey into consciousness will serve us well here again.

The spirituality of forgiveness.   We interpreted the first steps in world soul making in spiritual terms as learning to forgive. Indeed, they are steps in forgiving self and others, but they are rudimentary. This is the spiritual lesson of this fifth step in world soul making, balancing centers. From this new perspective, we begin to see how deep this process of letting go of our egocentric need to remain angry, judgmental, accusing, and so on will really go— and it is all the way, for our egocentricity fuels our illusions of power and control.

A further stretching or widening of ourselves is the purpose of this fifth step. To accomplish this goal we have to let go of our usual feeling of ourselves, for it's our routine feeling of ourselves that perpetuates the imbalance of our centers. In other words, we stay in compulsion because we know how we feel in compulsion, and maintaining our customary feeling of ourself becomes our definition of feeling okay and ready to live. Balanced people simply cannot have the same feeling of self as they used to have, because their awareness of self has widened. They lose their sense of self at one level and find it at another level of existence.

Though this step remains an interior one, the stimulus for such deep change always comes from outside self. It's other people, their words and actions, that will be the occasion for this stretching and widening of our concept of self. Consider, for example, the experience of being criticized in public for not accomplishing a task you said you would accomplish. Your reaction is an explosive tirade of criticism, anger, rage, or bitterness and sarcasm. Only when you stop yourself from such outbursts (whether they happen aloud or within) can you begin interior work.

First, you struggle to observe yourself. You notice thoughts, feelings, and reactions and how they proceed from either the Dominant Center or the Repressed Center. Doing so places a healthy distance between you and your feelings. As you calm down, a little bit of consciousness comes to bear on the situation. The feelings are not you; they are only a part of you.

Then you remember that you are the only one who can control your own response. "What," you ask, "is the cause in me of this response?" Invariably, the cause will be in your usual feeling of yourself. Either the criticism injured your customary feeling of yourself, or it is something you don't include in your habitual feeling of yourself. Either way, because the comment was critical, you have become upset and blamed the other person. Withdrawing the blame and doing your inner work is the first part of forgiveness. It's getting the octopus off your face, telling the old gossip to leave, evicting the starlings from the attic of your mind.

Then you can begin dealing with the issue. If what the person has said injures your usual feeling of yourself, you look at it to see where and how this evaluation might be true. You typically evaluate your performance on a scale between adequate and excellent, but you didn't realize these evaluations were so important to how you felt about yourself. By discovering those occasions when your performance doesn't meet standard and including them in your self-concept, you stretch yourself.

If what the person said isn't something you include in your habitual feeling of self, you know where to look for it—it's in your unconscious. Even though you may not immediately recognize it, you can be certain it's hidden there in some form because of your explosive response.

This inner work is the second and all-important part of forgiveness, for without it forgiveness doesn't last. The gracious words of forgiving are easily blown away by the force of our unconscious, and therefore untamed, emotion.

Here we begin to intuit how much will be required of us on this journey into world soul making. Our entire sense of self will be transformed, and therefore our discomfort will be intense. Now we come to know what it means to be born again in the spirit—it means widening ourselves and stretching our arms so that finally we can embrace the world. In that loving embrace we will find our destiny.

Touching the Center of Communion

In the previous steps we began the hard work of transformation. In this step we share that gift with others. As this movement begins in us, for the first time we are truly able to delight in other people because we are finally at peace with ourselves. You can't give what you haven't got. Now that we begin to recognize our own intrinsic dignity, we can respect other people's. As we forgive and love ourselves, we can forgive and love others.

In the language of the Enneagram, our centers of intelligence are more than balanced with one another; they are beginning to converge, and we are touching the creativity that transcends all. As we find communion within, the communion with others is transforming.

As the centers begin to converge, they create the fourth Center of Communion. In this step we begin to touch a transcendent level of existence. The fruit will be obvious and will be seen in acts of compassion, justice, mercy, and selflessness. As the centers converge, the basis of egocentricity crumbles, for it was founded upon our propensity to inflate one center over the other two.

This step is an incongruous union of exhilaration and discomfort. Because we've found the meaning of life, we feel more effective, dynamic, self-fulfilled, resilient, hopeful, and closer to our true destiny as a person.

Spiritually, what is happening is profound. Forgiveness is achieving a new level in us as it becomes natural. It is no longer something we *give,* as if we could choose to withhold it. It is no longer something we *do,* as if we need to make a choice for it. More and more, forgiveness becomes the nature of our being. A continual and dependable welcoming, receiving, accepting, relational style is the result.

Drawn forward by Love.　As we become bonded to humanity, our lives are marked by gratitude. But this is not all. Toward the end of this phase we begin to perceive—personally, experientially—the goal and meaning of it all. It is a revelation experienced and recorded from people of many diverse backgrounds.

Toward the end of his life, Jung was questioned by a reporter. "Do you believe in God?" the interviewer queried. "I don't have to believe," Jung responded confidently, "I *know.*"

In the final years of his life, Paul of Tarsus wrote words of similar meaning: "It is no longer I who live, it is Christ who lives in me."

In the last month of his life, the paleontologist and theologian Pierre Teilhard de Chardin wrote the final summary of his mystical-scientific vision for humanity. In it, he said,

> the universe has reached a higher level, where its . . . powers gradually assume the form of a fundamental affinity which links individuals to each other and to their transcendent Center. In us and around us the el-

ements of the world go on unceasingly personalizing themselves more and more, by acceding to a Term of unification; itself (so) personal that from this Term . . . there radiates and to this Term . . . there flows back all the essential Energy of the World. . . . What name must be given to such an influence? One only—Love; Love, the supreme form and the totalizing principle of human energy.[8]

Living in the Center of Communion

Having found unity and simplicity within, what is there inside one to diminish or distort the flow of life and love outward to all? As if carried on a great wave of loving, giving, connecting, and receiving, we cannot but speak and bring wisdom, touch and bring healing, listen and bring comfort, love and bring Love. For to live in the Center of Communion means to be drawn into the heart of God—to feel as God feels, to care as God cares, to be compassionate as God is compassionate, to love, heal, and forgive as God loves, heals, and forgives.

In this step there is an explosion of energy that shatters previously known boundaries and awakens our consciousness to a world without boundaries. As the illusions fall from our eyes, for the first time we really see: I am not living on this earth next to many brothers and sisters. I

---

[8]Pierre Teilhard de Chardin, *Building the Earth* (Wilkes-Barre, PA: Dimension Books, 1965), pp. 81–82.

am my sister! I *am* my brother! *"Nothing is precious save what is yourself in others and others in yourself.* In heaven, all things are but one. In heaven all is one."[9]

If it is the truth of heaven, this final phase of transformation calls us to make it true now. The works of justice and mercy, equality and compassion become our passion.

When my brother and my sister hurt, I hurt. When they thirst, I thirst, and when they starve, I starve. When they are bandaged and nourished, it is I who receive these gifts. When they are lonely, afraid, and oppressed, so am I. And when they are befriended, comforted, and freed, it is I who receive. Even as I give these gifts, I give them to myself, for I know no boundaries. *All become One.*

Years ago we heard of a woman who, with her husband, invited foreign exchange students to live with their family as the students attended the local university in Boulder, Colorado. One year a Japanese student arrived, and after he had lived with the family for a while, the woman invited him to take a ride with her one day into the mountains. As they roamed some mountain trails on foot, they began to talk more freely to each other. The young man was at first amazed at the beauty of the Colorado Rockies, but soon his feeling descended into anger at the beauty he saw when he compared it to the havoc America had wreaked on Japan at Hiroshima and Nagasaki.

The woman, who herself had visited Japan and seen the devastation, was deeply moved by the young man

---

[9]Pierre Teilhard de Chardin, *Hymn of the Universe* (New York: Harper & Row, 1961), p. 62.

and, wanting to extend her hand in more than friend-ship alone, told him of her sorrow at what had been done to his nation, asking his forgiveness. Remaining obsti-nate, the young Japanese turned his back on her.

Responding from the honesty she had long honed in herself, yet always keeping it relational, the woman be-came angry. She stooped down and plucked a wildflower from the ground as the student turned to watch her. Then she crushed the flower, opening a pod of seeds, scattering them broadly. "What will grow here?" she de-manded from him.

"More of the same flower," the student responded, slightly bewildered.

"And so it is for you and me. Without forgiveness, we live under the law, and we reap what we sow. At the end of the war, Japan reaped the harvest it had sown at Pearl Harbor. God knows what harvest America will reap from Hiroshima and Nagasaki—unless we stop this foolishness with forgiveness and healing."

And so that day, an American homemaker and a Japanese student knelt on a mountainside and prayed for forgiveness and healing for themselves and for their two wounded nations. Who knows what harvest will be reaped from that moment when love was made real and became visible on the earth!

Living in the Center of Communion, even if just for a moment on a mountainside, means being a conduit of the divine into this world. It means doing our part to unite the world of spirit with the world of matter. Having found the power of self in selflessness, we reach for the stars and find they have made a home inside us.

When we find a home in the Center of Communion, we have stretched our arms to embrace the world. The work of justice and equality in the world community becomes ours. All people, all cultures, all the wonders of creation find a home in us, and we find a home in them. Our values are universal, and we are universal in our love.

What is inside replicates itself outside. If we live in unity, we create unity, and we reap the rewards of unity. We live in peace. We live in God, God lives in us, and *all become One.*

The Golden Swan

Throughout these latter pages we have written of the bonding of our three centers of intelligence working in harmony and of how, when unity among them comes about, we give birth to the transcendent fourth—the Center of Communion. Yet, we have also been weaving into the tapestry of these ideas the values and images of another dimension of reality. This reality, though not easily perceived in our daily living, is, even in its obscurity, no less important. This is the mystery of the Golden Swan.

The swan is the largest of the water fowl, with a wingspan that reaches from six to ten feet. On the waters of the harsh northern climates, the swan spends the spring and summer strengthening its wings enough to lift its large body off the water and learn to fly, lest it remain weak and be left to die on the frozen ponds of winter.

In the swan we find one symbol that speaks to us of all that this book contains. Its long, phallic neck and soft, rounded body are the union of masculine and feminine out of which a new era is being born. Its two powerful wings are the force by which it ascends into the heavens, speaking allegorically to us of forgiveness and love.

Although these four parts of the swan are not in perfect symmetry, they work in unity as one. Unity within—not perfect symmetry or androgyny—is what will lead to harmony and peace in the world. The two wings of the swan—forgiveness and love—grow in balanced proportion. If we fail to work through issues of forgiveness, any belief that a wing of love will grow is an illusion. Instead, the truth is, we are choosing to die on the frozen ponds of resentment.

Through intuition, the swan receives guidance for its long migration from northernmost to southernmost terrains. The flight of the swan inspires our imaginations to reach for the heights of beauty, grace, and power it represents. It inspires the Divine Child within each of us to want to fly, to soar to the heights.

Wings stretched in flight, their greatness embraces the world. Through all these associations as well as its connection with singing the melody of the soul, the swan evokes a desire for spirituality in us all.

The Golden Swan tells us of the illumination and transcendence of the divine layering into our earthly reality—God not separate and above, but intermingling, penetrating, luminescent and present, glimmering through created reality. The pure gold of Love permeates all. That is why we place the swan in the middle of the Enneagram.

This is the God who shines from within and draws all creation together. Calling and empowering every person to unity, God radiates and to God there flows back the joy of unity. God empowers us to be like God. The power to give away power—by this shall we know God and all who love God.

This Love draws us forward to a new era in the twenty-first century. As we make our souls in the midst of everyday life we strengthen them to carry this spiritual presence into our world. With it a new era will be born, and all of creation will be drawn toward the final destiny of oneness.

April 29, 1992—Simi Valley, California. The four police officers accused of using undue force in the beating of Rodney King are found not guilty by a jury of their peers.

April 29, 1992—Los Angeles, California. Riots break out in many parts of the city, and the forces of violence run rampant. Brutal beatings, shootings, fires, and looting control the city.

April 30, 1992—Washington, D.C. In a speech to the nation, President George Bush states emphatically, "Murder and destruction in the city of Los Angeles must be stopped."

April 30, 1992—Washington, D.C. The President declares a state of emergency in the city of Los Angeles and orders four thousand National Guard troops to assist city and state police in establishing order.

April 30, 1992—New York City. On the evening news on NBC, commentator John Chancellor declares, "For a decade our politicians have sidestepped racial issues."

April 30, 1992—Los Angeles, California. It was reported that African-American actor Greg Alan-Williams intervened in the beating of a white trucker by African Americans in Los Angeles and saved the man's life, asserting, "This is *not* a racial issue. This is a *human* issue."

Are we beginning to reevaluate our values, institutions, and governments? Are we going to call our leaders—political, spiritual, and cultural—to account? Are we calling ourselves to account for our personal lives and our contributions to family, community, and culture?

We are being drawn irresistibly toward the millennium. What is my choice? What is your choice? What is our choice? What will we choose? Will we consciously or unconsciously perpetrate violence, or will be become world soul makers?

We are indeed living in exciting and perilous times.

The entire world is holy. In this way, the power of beauty has no limits, and repression finds its denunciation. . . . If we have clear ideas about the presence of God in humanity, then we will be more and more convinced that the world is the temple of the Spirit and that the Spirit passes through the people, through the human spirit, moving into a deeper and more profound communion.[10]

> *When all become One*
> *The riddle is solved.*

---

[10]Leonardo Boff, a Brazilian theologian, in an address he delivered at the University of São Paulo in October 1991, translated and published in *National Catholic Reporter* 28, no. 23 (April 10, 1992), p. 2.